Deeper

HEART TO HEART
WITH HOLY SPIRIT

A Journey of Discovery Toward Healing,
Restoration, Identity, and Destiny

DEANNA OELKE

Deeper – Heart to Heart with Holy Spirit

© 2018 by Deanna Oelke

Published by Deeper Ministries

deeperministries@shaw.ca

www.deeperministries.ca

Cover Design and Layout by: ChristianAuthorsGetPaid.com

Editor: Cheryl Regier

Zachariah House

zachariahhouseofhelps@gmail.com

Unless otherwise indicated, all Scripture quotations are taken from the Holy Bible, New Living Translation, copyright © 1996, 2004, 2007 by Tyndale House Foundation. Used by permission of Tyndale House Publishers, Inc., Carol Stream, IL 60188. All rights reserved.

Scripture quotations marked (NIV) are taken from the Holy Bible, New International Version®, NIV®. Copyright © 1973, 1978, 1984, 2011 by Biblica, Inc.™ Used by permission of Zondervan. All rights reserved worldwide. www.zondervan.com. The "NIV" and "New International Version are trademarks registered in the United States Patent and Trademark Office by Biblica, Inc.™

Scripture quotations marked (NKJV) are taken from the New King James Version®. Copyright © 1982 by Thomas Nelson, Inc. Used by permission. All rights reserved.

Scripture quotations marked (AMPCE) are taken from the Amplified® Bible, Copyright © 1954, 1958, 1962, 1964, 1965, 1987 by The Lockman Foundation. Used by permission.

Scripture quotations are from The Holy Bible, English Standard Version® (ESV®), copyright © 2001 by Crossway, a publishing ministry of Good News Publishers. Used by permission. All rights reserved.

Printed in the United States of America

ISBN: 978-0-9952762-2-2

What Leaders are Saying

About Deeper

"Prophecy wasn't new to me, as I grew up in a context where it was taught and practiced – the good, bad, and everything in between. I knew prophecy was a God-given gift, but I found myself walking through long, dormant seasons. I placed restrictions on myself, believing a lie that I had to be in a charismatic environment to operate in this gifting. I was so very wrong. I craved a community that understood the prophetic nature of the Body of Christ. I found this from the first moment I met Deanna and journeyed through the Deeper experience. I received the most biblically sound teaching and practice of prophecy I had ever been exposed to. Deanna pulls from Scripture, revelation, and life experience. Her gift and wisdom take you on a journey of what it truly means to hear and obey the voice of God in a way that brings glory to God and exhorts others. The season spent with Deeper served as a catalyst in my life. This experience unlocked areas in my spiritual journey that had been closed for many years. I walked away equipped to disciple others to operate in a New Testament, biblical approach to prophecy."

Travis Wilkins, Lead Pastor
Centre Street Church, Airdrie Campus
(Airdrie, Alberta, Canada)

"Deeper has dramatically changed my relationship with my Heavenly Father. It opened the door for a two-way communication with Him. Hearing the voice of God for others and myself is a beautiful gift from above that is now a part of my everyday life. Not a day goes by I don't hear, sense, or feel His presence."

Reagan Bowers, Replenish Ministry
Centre Street Church
(Calgary, Alberta, Canada)

"When invited to attend Deeper, I knew instantly that this was God's answer to my cry for help to learn about my spiritual gifts. Deanna is a strong pioneer who teaches with authenticity, vulnerability, wisdom, and grace. She offers a perfect blend of solid, biblical grounding with ample opportunity to practice exploring the gifts God has given to each of us. What struck me most profoundly through Deeper was the myriad of ways in which God bestows His gifts. It made me realize how vital it is for each of us in the Body to operate in our giftedness. I encourage every believer to gather a few trusted people around you and work your way through the Deeper materials together. I promise you will grow in your appreciation and love of God. You will learn about who you are and what you specifically bring to the Body of Christ. You will grow in confidence in living life more fully, being transformed and encouraged to press on."

Andrea Bye, Life Coach
Andrea Bye Life Coaching

"In going through Deeper, I learned how to recognize, hear, and test God's voice in a safe place. It was exciting to understand what I have been experiencing for years in communicating with God. Deeper has changed my life."

Valerie Hopman, Monday Night Evangelism
Centre Street Church (Calgary, Alberta, Canada)

"If you've ever tried to tune in to a radio station from a remote location or watch television with rabbit ears, you will understand static – scratchy, fuzzy sounds that distort and even cover up the picture or sound. My relationship with God was distorted by static. I was having trouble hearing God's voice. I was having trouble seeing His plans for me. The Deeper course gave me the space and tools to eliminate that static so that my Heavenly Father's voice was clear. As a pastor, Deeper significantly enhanced my ministry by giving me the ability and confidence to use my prophetic voice to share God's love and encouragement with my friends and parishioners."

Jen Snow, Children and Families Pastor
Calgary First Church of the Nazarene
(Calgary, Alberta, Canada)

What Participants are Saying

About Deeper

"It is my great pleasure and honor to endorse Deanna's work with Deeper. Through the teaching in Deeper, the world of the prophetic came alive in my life. By celebrating the prophetic gift in me, Deanna taught me how to readily access and share Holy Spirit in a new and fresh way. My life and the lives of those around me have been deeply enriched. Thank you!"

Shari S.

"Deanna's teaching in Deeper has helped me take my relationship with God deeper and wider than I ever could have imagined. Learning to hear Him speak to me and for others has been such a precious gift. It has enabled me to serve the Body of Christ in new ways and to walk closer with Him each day. Deanna and Deeper have been such incredible blessings in my life!"

Natalie D.

"Through Deeper, my relationship with Father God and Jesus Christ was beautifully transformed as I learned practical ways to abide in Jesus and enjoy His loving presence. I learned ways to truly listen to Holy Spirit. I discovered that, not only has God been speaking to me all my life, but also His written Word has opened up to me in amazing, new ways. Praise God!"

Sophie I.

"Hearing God's voice should be core doctrine in our churches. Deeper reinforced the biblical truth that God still speaks in a variety of ways, and it equipped me with "conversation starters" like entering His presence through worship and asking Him specific questions. I was often amazed by how quickly, clearly, and personally He answered. In living life, self-doubt can get in the way, but there is nothing so reassuring as hearing and trusting God's voice. He speaks love that envelops me in tenderness, comfort, and security. He is all I need, and I want to know Him more."

Carolyn K.

"I was far from God and going through the motions when I came to Deeper. The worship provided an atmosphere for God to touch my life. My distance from God was caused by pride, sin, a judgmental attitude, and a belief that I wasn't far from God, but He was far from me. As the weeks progressed, I came to realize God wanted to speak to me, and I was highly valued. The prophetic guidelines of comfort, encouragement, and strength made the place safe. The personal words from God through the prophetic gift from others touched me and broke off the lies I had believed about God."

Bill H.

"I have known Jesus as my personal Savior for many years. For most of that time, it never occurred to me that God wanted to, and already was, speaking to me. What a blessing to have Deanna's, biblical teaching open my heart and ears to Holy Spirit's voice. What a joy to have a name for the sweet voice and presence that has been there through my journey and to become more fully aware of His role in my life. I am thankful for the help and guidance I received through Deeper as I continue in my spiritual journey."

Rachel B.

"I felt like a pioneer in my prophetic gifting. Deanna's teaching provided me with a solid, biblical foundation for my journey in the prophetic. Deeper helped me recognize the variety of ways God speaks to encourage, comfort, and strengthen others and myself and to thrive in God's Kingdom. After some practice, I noticed how energized I felt in my gift of prophecy as it demonstrated God's love in a relational way. My journey in the prophetic has greatly increased from Deanna's instruction, and I look forward to more of her books!"

Kim B.

"I was privileged to be a part of Deanna's Deeper group at our church where she taught the principles in this book. To see and hear others move in the prophetic was an amazing and deeply encouraging thing. One of the standout memories was hearing Deanna point out that, in 1 Corinthians chapters 12 and 14, we are told to eagerly desire the gifts of the Spirit. Hearing her tell of reading about the gifts in the Bible years earlier and passionately saying "I want that!" was eye opening to me. The amazing prophetic gift she now has is a result of her journey of passionately desiring to be more and more filled with Holy Spirit and the gifts He gives. I pray that, as you read this book, your hunger for Holy Spirit and to be used by Him will be stirred."

Al K.

Dedication

I would like to dedicate this book to my parents for being such a beautiful example of living daily in the Christian faith.

Thank you, Mom and Dad, for being my first spiritual teachers. I am grounded in the Word of God and in my spiritual disciplines because of your teaching and training. You modeled to me how to live an authentic Christian life, and I am forever grateful. Thank you for your love and willingness to support and help me over the years. I am blessed for having you as my parents.

Acknowledgements

I would like to thank my pastor, Kervin Raugust, for his willingness to work with me on this book.

Thank you, Kervin, for investing your time, not only in advising me and reviewing this book but also for contributing to my personal growth. I have never journeyed with someone that models living in the Word of God and in the Spirit of God as gracefully as you do. I count it a privilege to be under your leadership, mentorship, and counsel.

Foreword

"I am thirsty!"

Thirsting is an image the Psalmist used to express the deepest yearning of his soul. "As the deer pants for streams of water, so my soul pants for you, my God. My soul thirsts for God, for the living God." (Psalm 42:1-2a, NIV) Jesus had soul thirsts as well. He cried out from the cross, "I am thirsty." (John 19:28) Thirst is a normal craving of the heart. "I am thirsty" is a confession of desire and a declaration of destiny!

The problem with cravings is they can be quenched in ways that satisfy but do not nourish. Think of it this way. The roots of a tree naturally seek water. If roots tap into a pure water source, the tree flourishes. But if even one root finds its way to a polluted water source, the tree withers. A withering tree is stunted in its growth and produces little or no fruit. So it is with our soul thirsts.

Let's go with Jesus for a moment to the well in Samaria. Can you see Him sitting there in conversation with the woman who came to fetch water? Overhearing the conversation, we hear Jesus saying something like, "Imagine, dear woman, what it would be like for you to drink water which satisfies your thirst so much that *you would never thirst again*? Imagine what your life would be like if *you became a source of living water*? Imagine!" (John 4:13-14) So she imagined and panted out, "Give me this water..." (John 4:15)

There is panting going on, and Deanna has heard it. It is the panting that says, "I am tired of performance-based religion. I am tired of striving to go deeper in intimacy with Jesus. I am tired of hearing the diminishing voice of 'you are not good enough'. I am tired of living in bondage to lies.

I am thirsty!" Deanna heard this panting in her own soul, and it carried her to Jesus. She discovered the path that leads to freedom and that Jesus has something to say to His panting followers. That is why Deanna wrote this book. Her invitation is to drink deeply of Jesus. He is the pure and living source of water that promises a life of freedom and abundance!

Deanna has descended from deep unto deep in her relationship with Jesus. In her decent, she has discovered the simple pathway to hearing the voice of God. This is a safe pathway based solidly on a biblical foundation and supported by years of personal experiences with Holy Spirit of Jesus. Under assignment, Deanna has written a book that will carefully guide you to discovering and following the pathway to, not only hearing God's voice for yourself, but also hearing God's voice for others.

To all who pant for more, Jesus says, "Come drink deeply of Me, thirsty one! Learn to hear My voice and see how I show up for you, in you, and through you! Drink deeply, and you will discover the joy of being a source of living water for others!"

Kervin Raugust is the President of the Evangelical Missionary Church of Canada and served as the Executive Pastor of Centre Street Church in Calgary, Alberta. He is a student of prophetic ministry and has benefited immensely from the mentoring of Deanna Oelke.

Table of Contents

Deep calls to deep
in the roar of your waterfalls
all your waves and breakers
have swept over me.
By day the Lord directs his love,
at night his song is with me —
a prayer to the God of my life.

(Psalm 42:7-8, NIV)

Introduction

Jesus said in (John 10:10)

"The thief [Satan] comes only to steal and kill and destroy; I have come that they may have life, and have it to the full." (NIV)

Our life on earth is not just to survive on this side of eternity. This promise of abundant life from Jesus is a rich, satisfying life. This promise is for you! You may be recognizing that Satan has killed parts of your life, stolen and destroyed parts of who you were created to be. Your life is not over and does not end here! You have a promise: "But I, Jesus, have come that YOU might have abundant life!"

I have experienced living with Satan's vice grip on my spiritual and emotional being. Now, I live in the reality of freedom, healing, and wholeness in Jesus Christ. I have been released from spiritual and emotional bondage from my childhood and been brought to the place of personal restoration, living in the fullness of who Father God created me to be. My healing took time, and the losses were great. But I emerged changed and transformed – a new, upgraded Deanna. This is what Holy Spirit does: He is in the business of supernaturally transforming lives. This is my story and my victory song.

Deeper was created as I began to pull together the spiritual principles I learned over the years in my healing and restoration journey and in my journey of discovering my identity and destiny in Christ. In the first part of

1

Deeper, I will personally share my journey from emotional bondage into healing and wholeness. My desire in doing this is not so that you can know me better, but it is so that you can get to know my Jesus, my Heavenly Father, and my Holy Spirit better. I hope and pray that you will see their kind, healing, tender heart towards me during my healing journey. My journey to freedom flowed out of relationship – learning how to love the Lord my God with all my heart, soul, mind, and strength (Mark 12:29-30). Learning how to love God was something that did not come naturally to me and was something that I needed to learn how to do. Holy Spirit led me in loving God and taught me very personally.

The second part of *Deeper* is a practical guide in how to journey with Holy Spirit – a step-by-step for listening to Him and learning from Him. Two of the main tools that were significant in leading me into my personal freedom was, number one, learning how to hear God's voice for myself, and number two, being in a community that could hear God's voice for others through the gift of prophecy. For this reason, learning how to hear God's voice and learning how to operate in the gift of prophecy will be a major focus of the teaching in *Deeper*.

As you journey through *Deeper – Heart to Heart with Holy Spirit*, either on your own or with a biblical community, my prayer is that you come to know, practically and through experience, the love of Christ which far surpasses mere knowledge. May you be made complete with all the fullness of life and power that comes from God. My hope is that God will accomplish infinitely more than you could ever ask or imagine in you and through you! (Ephesians 3:18-20)

2

Beauty for Ashes

Original painting by Deanna Oelke

Jesus gave me "beauty for ashes". (Isaiah 61:3)

This painting is the first in a series on Isaiah 61. The lotus flower grows in muddy, murky water representing beauty growing in the midst of difficult circumstances. The roots of the flower are strong, sinewy, and intertwined, representing a strength of relationship with Jesus. The background alludes to brokenness and difficulties, yet the coloring transforms it into beauty.

God has made everything beautiful in its time (Ecclesiastes 3:11). When we allow Jesus to touch our 'ashes' and work within us, we can't help but be transformed. The results are beyond what we could attain in our own human strength. The results are supernatural.

3

Chapter 1

My Journey into Healing

Emotional Bondage

Jesus gave me *"beauty for [my] ashes, the oil of joy for mourning, the garment of praise for [my] spirit of heaviness."*(Isaiah 61:3, NKJV)

I am a living testimony of Jesus' ability to supernaturally transform a life of ashes, mourning, and heaviness into beauty, joy, and praise. By all appearances, it looked like my life was great. I was raised in a Christian home where my parents lived their Christianity authentically and were a great example to me in how to live out spiritual disciplines and a life of integrity. We regularly attended a Baptist church where I learned and practiced multiple, spiritual disciplines: reading and studying the Bible, praying, and being involved in our church community. I accepted Jesus as my Lord and Saviour at the age of nine. My desire was to honour God with my life, and the choices I made throughout my life reflected my heart. I was a good Christian girl raised in a good Christian home. It all looked great from the outside, but this was not the reality of my internal world.

As a child and a teenager, I lived in constant, emotional turmoil. I struggled with depression as a child and with suicidal thoughts as a teenager. I did not know it at the time, but a demonic spirit had established a foothold within my inner being, attaching to my emotions just as my personality was emerging as a toddler. Later in my life, I discovered this demonic spirit was present in my family line as a result of generational sin (Exodus 20:5). This generational sin provided the foothold for the demonic, giving it the opportunity to oppress me and bind up my emotions. Although God had designed me to have a breadth and an expanse of feelings, this demonic hold on my emotions left me experiencing only a fraction of my feelings. Over the years, this spirit established an even stronger grip over my emotions based on lies, verbal pronouncements, curses, and my own personal sin. This systematic layering of Satan's plans for my life allowed him to hold me in emotional bondage. Satan's activity was done slowly, silently, and with deception, causing him and his agenda to remain hidden for years.

The influence of this demonic spirit on my emotional health caused my personality to be misshaped. I was a very shy, withdrawn, serious, and socially awkward child. I could not fully feel all my emotions and had difficulty emotionally engaging with people and with God. Fortunately, God hardwired my personality for faith, and I was able to live my Christian walk in pure faith without ever feeling an emotional connection of love with Jesus. I knew in my head that I loved Jesus. I participated in my spiritual disciplines simply because I knew they were good for me and that I would spiritually grow through their practice. Rarely, however, did I feel motivated by love.

Since I could not feel the love of Jesus, it perpetuated the thinking that I needed to *do* things for Jesus to be worthy of receiving God's love. My relationship with Jesus became connected to doing, not being. The more I served Jesus, practiced my spiritual disciplines, and obeyed the Bible, the better I would feel as a Christian. I subsequently viewed this as success. The weeks or seasons that I would be unmotivated by my Bible reading and prayer would push me into shame and self-condemnation. As a result, I would feel like I was failing as a Christian.

Living in Demonic Bondage

As a teenager, I recognized that I was in emotional torment, but I could not pinpoint the cause of such pain to anything external in my life. Although I did not like myself, I had no reason to believe the feelings I was experiencing indicated that I could be any different than I was. So unfortunately, I accepted my misshapen personality as my reality, shutdown emotions and all, and thought that this was just how God had created me.

My self-hate eventually manifested in an eating disorder in my early twenties, which Satan used to draw me into a deeper level of bondage. After years of living with my eating disorder, I finally recognized that I needed help and sought out a Christian counsellor. She counselled me to see myself in a positive light and gave me tools for living life well as a young woman. Specifically, she taught me to take

7

my thoughts of self-hate captive to the obedience of Christ and to speak and think positively about myself instead. I also learned to take responsibility for my actions and to establish healthy physical, emotional, and spiritual habits in my life. God used this period of counselling to show me where I was sinning in my actions, and Holy Spirit led me to repentance. As I implemented these spiritual and emotional tools, I walked into freedom from the eating disorder.

As I moved into the next season of my life, continuing to take my thoughts captive and repenting as Holy Spirit revealed sins in my life, I experienced God's healing on certain levels related to my emotions and my personality. The depression that I had lived with all my life was finally gone. I started to feel more of my emotions, and God began to free me from aspects of the demonic layering that Satan had established in my life years earlier. The root of those strongholds of generational sin remained, but I did not feel the full effect of their demonic grip on my life. Instead, God covered me with His hand of grace, for He desired me to experience my true identity and personality. I began to get a taste of who God had created me to be and, for the first time in my life, I liked myself! Contrary to what I had believed in the past, I started to see that I was bold, confident, and passionate. Furthermore, I discovered that I had the gift of leadership. My emotions and personality were undergoing a transformation with these revelations.

Within a few months, I met my future husband and started my teaching career. I quickly realized that I was skilled as a teacher, and I thrived within the Christian school that I taught at. Experiencing success in my teaching career fuelled my performance-based tendencies – one of those deep-rooted, unhealthy mentalities – and increased my pride and independence. God knew I still needed emotional healing and spiritual freedom in these areas. In His wisdom, He knew the best path for me to step into the fullness of my identity.

Holy Spirit

In this season, as a young wife and teacher, a friend of mine began going to a new church in our city. I visited her church, and there, I saw and experienced the gifts of Holy Spirit in operation. I had never experienced or seen this growing up in my Baptist church. I did not understand what I was witnessing, but I could sense the presence of Holy Spirit. My curiosity drew me into their community.

My husband, Harvey, came with me to this new church a couple of times, but he did not share my excitement. I am bold in my nature, whereas my husband is cautious. I was fully ready to switch churches; however, Harvey was not. We had many lengthy discussions as a result. Neither of us was willing to flex in favour of the other. Then, God very clearly spoke to me, "Deanna, I want you to submit to Harvey. Stay where you are in your current church, and I will teach you about Holy Spirit." Problem solved.

My knowledge and understanding of Holy Spirit was limited. As a young girl growing up in a traditional Baptist church, I was taught that Holy Spirit existed, but He remained quite mysterious in my Baptist culture. He was mentioned, but I certainly didn't learn about His ways or who He was. I primarily learned about Jesus and Father God. I especially loved Jesus, and He was my friend. Father felt more removed and His presence a little ominous. But Holy Spirit... He seemed almost irrelevant. Yes, He was my helper, my comforter, my guide, but so, also, was Jesus to me. As I matured as a Christian, I found that the common explanation of Holy Spirit's function was to act as my conscience.

As Father God taught me about Holy Spirit, He led me to books, courses, and conferences. This knowledge provided a strong, biblical basis for me to understand Holy Spirit. As I embarked on this journey to personally know Holy Spirit, I realized I was hungry for Him and His ways. I felt like He was a new friend, and yet He was very familiar. I also realized that He had always been with me even though I had treated Him like a silent partner. As I consciously engaged with Him, I came to know Him on a much deeper level. I began to discover Holy Spirit as a unique member of the Holy Trinity. He was far more than just my conscience.

Learning to Hear God and Holy Spirit's Voice through Journaling

After seven years of a wonderful, teaching career and becoming the mother to a beautiful baby girl, I accepted a job as a principal. This position was difficult for me, forcing me to rely on God's strength instead of my own. God had to show me the pride in my life. He also revealed that I was more concerned about how others viewed me than how He viewed me. To process my difficult experiences and emotions during this time, I began to journal.

Journaling was not new to me. What *was* new was writing down what I was sensing God saying to me. My process was as follows:

- I would journal my thoughts and feelings about the situation, expressing them as if I were talking to God. No matter how raw and unprocessed my feelings were, I would write them down. This ended up being healthy in and of itself, for it taught me that I didn't need to have my emotions or my situation all together before I came to God. Instead, I could come before Him with all my mess, my uncensored feelings, and my heart's deepest desires.

- When I was done expressing myself, I would wait and listen for God to speak to me through my thoughts. Then, I would write down the first thought or impression that would come into my head, choosing in the moment not to allow my mind to stop the thoughts by thinking, *"Is this me, or is this God?"* I would simply write the thoughts down as if God were speaking to me. Sometimes, I would just begin by writing, *"My child..."* and then write whatever came to my mind.

- After I sensed the thoughts from God were done, I would go back and ensure that all of the 'God thoughts' lined up with the truth of the Bible and the character of God. This was my test. I knew my Bible well as a good Baptist Christian, and therefore, I knew that God's spoken word would never contradict His written Word or His character.

Occasionally, I would instantly sense that the 'God thoughts' I was writing down were truly from Him. In those moments, I could hear the truth of the words and could feel the healing and comfort that came with them. This 'inner witness' was the 'good fruit' that confirmed to me that God was indeed speaking through my thoughts as I waited on Him. In other journaling times, I would not immediately sense if it was God speaking to me or if it was my own thoughts. For these times, if the thoughts I had written down lined up with the Bible and God's character,

11

then I would leave them and come back to them, rereading them after some time had gone by. I often found that, after a few weeks or months, I had indeed heard from God, especially when events came to pass. I experienced much good fruit in these precious, journaling times with the Lord – love, joy, peace, patience, goodness, and kindness.

Journal Entry: October 2000

Dear Lord, You are so good and awesome. I thank you for giving me the desire to serve You and for fuelling my passion to minister with my teachers and my student leaders. Help me to be the leader that You desire, that pleases You, that is humble and contrite of heart, that is quick to listen and slow to anger, that is willing to admit being wrong. I want to be sensitive to the people around me. Give me wisdom as I deal with parents, teachers, and students, for all that You are teaching me and for the ways that You are growing me. I want to constantly chase after You. You are most worthy of my praise.

God thoughts: "My child, you have come so far. Be obedient to Me. Love Me. Stay close to Me and hear My voice. The Shepherd knows His sheep, and they know Him by the sound of His voice."

Lord, I want to know Your voice so that, when the world is screaming so loudly at me, I can hear You and know You. You know me and call me by my name. I want to know You more!

God thoughts: "Obey Me, trust Me, I will feed you. Hold My Word close to your heart and obey Me. Be radical in your obedience. Obey Me, Deanna, and love Me. I trust you and want you to obey Me. Be the best you that you can be! Use your gifts to honour and glorify My name."

Refuel me, Lord, and refine me. You are good. Thank you for the time and effort and patience that You have put into this old, clay pot. I bless Your name above all names, for You are worthy to be praised!

I was learning a key step in how to have a two-way relationship with my Maker. It was out of this relationship that my healing began. God is called *The Word*, and I discovered that *The Word* liked to talk to me very personally in the moment that I needed to hear from Him. My Christianity took a positive step away from performing a 'To Do' list out of religious duty and obligation. Instead, I moved towards a relationship of speaking and listening to God and living my life in response to Him out of that intimacy. I was learning how to 'be' in relationship with God.

Through my 'being' with God, I came to understand that my job as a principal was serving the purpose of training me to become a better leader. I sensed that He had a future task for me that required a far greater woman than who I presently was. Thus, I needed to yield to God as He worked in my life to build my character and prepare me for the plans that He had for me (Jeremiah 29:11). God saw my life from His eternal perspective. He was willing to take whatever time was necessary to grow my character to match His assignment for me.

Fear of Intimacy

After two years of working as a principal, I was delighted to be able to stay home with my two children (Janessa and Caleb) and focus on being a full-time mom. This also gave me more time to focus on developing my relationship with God. This change, as welcome as it was, really pushed me out of my comfort zone.

Being a full-time mom was a completely different rhythm of life than what I was used to. I was busy physically, but mentally I was not. I had lots of time to think. In addition, the spoken approval of my 'doing' that I had experienced in my successful teaching career was gone. During this time, Holy Spirit worked to a greater level of undoing my performance mentality.

In response to Holy Spirit's work, I began to realize just how much my worth, value, and significance had been tied to what I accomplished. I could not see tangible accomplishments in my responsibilities as a mom in the short-term. Holy Spirit allowed things to bubble to the surface within me during this time to point out deep-seated issues that I didn't even know were there. This was a season of deep refining.

Within this change of rhythm for our family, I was noticing things about my relationship with Harvey that I wanted to see improved as well. As I examined our relationship, I could clearly see what Harvey needed to change. I found that nagging accomplished nothing positive in my marriage, so I decided to pray regarding my concerns and have Holy Spirit show Harvey what he needed to do. I had assumed that he was the problem.

One night while I was in the middle of praying for Harvey, Holy Spirit clearly spoke to me, *"You fear intimacy with men."* As soon as He spoke this, I felt the truth of this statement deep within my spirit, and I began to uncontrollably weep. In my mind, I did not understand. *"How did this happen? Am I the problem in my marriage? What do I do about this?"* Even with all my questions, I did know that this statement by Holy Spirit was very true.

God was revealing a deep, emotional problem within me. I instantly comprehended that my fear of intimacy had affected not only my relationship with Harvey, but my relationship with Father God as well. Out of the Trinity, Father was the most difficult for me to understand. My fear had led to me becoming emotionally disconnected from Him. This dysfunction trickled down to other relationships in my life.

Emotional Disconnect

As I reflected on my fear of intimacy, I noticed that I found it very difficult to emotionally connect, not just with Harvey, but with both of my children as well. I knew in my head that I loved them, but I could not feel the emotional connection of love for them. I also had difficulty in receiving unconditional love from them. I would protect myself by holding them at an emotional distance. I could not understand why I felt the need to protect myself from the people that I loved the most. My emotional disconnect was a puzzle, and it deeply grieved me.

I knew that something deep within my emotions needed healing, but I had no idea how to proceed. Yet, Holy Spirit knew, and He began to lead me. He first taught me how to live in the first and greatest commandment:

"Love the Lord your God with all your heart and with all your soul and with all your strength."
(Deuteronomy 6:5, NIV)

15

Worship

I did not want to stay in a place of fearing intimacy with Father God. I desired to be emotionally and spiritually connected with Him. Understanding that fear is a demonic spirit that behaves like a bully, I recognized that Satan would have me shrink back, stay in a place of fear (submit to it), and remain emotionally distant from Father God. The great thing about knowing what the enemy wanted to do in my life is that it also gave me the insight into what God intended for me, which was the exact opposite. To live free from fear, God wanted me to take steps to walk through that fear and foster emotional intimacy with Him.

To achieve this purpose, Holy Spirit led me to make worship a part of my daily routine. The Bible is full of verses about praise and worship. Learning how to be a worshipper taught me two key things: how to 'be' with God in relationship and how to foster intimacy.

I am a creative person, so simply singing worship songs bored me after a short time. My children were preschool and toddler age and constantly around me. I knew I needed to involve them in my worship time if I wanted to make this a daily discipline. So, I made simple worship flags from embroidery hoops with long ribbons tied to them and bought instruments for the children. I pulled together a selection of worship songs that I liked, including ones that the children liked as well. Spending time worshipping the Lord through dance, movement, and singing became a part of our daily routine.

Naptime in our home meant free time for me. I began to pick up my brushes and paint again. Having a creative outlet has always fulfilled something within me, but as I painted, I would feel so guilty. I thought, *"I have free time that I should be spending with God and not selfishly on myself. What kind of a Christian am I that I cannot even desire to spend time with God when I have the opportunity?"* And performance Christianity reared its ugly head once again.

In one particular, guilt-ridden, painting session, I heard Holy Spirit speak to me, *"Why don't you play worship music while you paint and invite Me into your time?"* Wow! Painting could be an act of worship! I experienced such freedom from shame and guilt with this statement. As I worshipped and painted with God, Jesus, and Holy Spirit, I sensed that they were saying that they created me to be an artist, and my art was an expression of worship as I involved them in the creative process. My joy in my painting and in worshipping them was reciprocated by their joy in me being who Father created me to be. My art became an assured avenue for the Lord to speak to me and give me creative ideas. Eventually, I started a business of painting murals and spiritual paintings.

Devotional Box

Habits of performance in Christianity can take a while to undo. My spiritual disciplines of reading the Bible and doing my devotions were good, but my motive behind doing them was very wrong. My motive in reading the Bible was to cross it off of my Christian 'to do' list rather than reading the Bible to get to know God better and foster relationship.

I remember being on a roll with my devotions and my Bible reading. I had done them every day for weeks! I was so proud of myself! One evening, as soon as my Bible closed, I heard God say to me, *"I have not been in any of your devotions. You have missed Me completely."* I was shocked! I was doing all the right things but completely

17

missing Him. Apparently, He had an opinion on how I was 'doing' relationship with Him.

God revealed that His intention was to teach me how to change my devotional time with Him into a time of true relationship building. Over the next few years Jesus spoke this verse to me often:

Then Jesus said, "Come to me, all of you who are weary and carry heavy burdens, and I will give you rest. Take my yoke upon you. Let me teach you, because I am humble and gentle at heart, and you will find rest for your souls. For my yoke is easy to bear, and the burden I give you is light." (Matthew 11:28-30)

I had experienced the heavy burden that performance-based Christianity had on my life. Wearied under the weight of this load I carried, I was willing to rest and learn from Jesus. But, how would I do this?

Journal Entry: October 2002

A word that You have spoken to me twice in the past three weeks is "Rest". Lord, I don't know how to rest or to wait well. I want to learn what it means to rest in You. How can I do this, and how can I wait well? I feel that I have done some 'good things' in my own strength. I want to obey You. I want to walk in Your will. Thank you for placing this desire in my heart. Remind me to stay here. My heart is to honour and glorify You. Show me when I stray or when pride is creeping in. Strengthen me with the power of Your Holy Spirit.

Father: "You are My child, and I adore you. I treasure you. I see your heart. I want you to just 'be' not 'do'. Obey Me. I love you. Rest in Me and enjoy My presence. Delight yourself in Me, and I will give you the desires of your heart."

My desire, Lord, is to have a true, intimate, two-way relationship with You.

Father: "Seek Me, and you will find Me if you seek Me with all your heart."

I began to listen to Holy Spirit before entering into my quiet times with Him, asking Him what He wanted it to look like. Holy Spirit began to draw me out of my 'devotional box', redefining what our times together should look like. I realized how fun Holy Spirit, Jesus, and Father God could be! Sometimes, Holy Spirit would tell me to take a walk and engage with Him in nature. Other times, He would communicate how tired He could see that I was and call me to spend time just sitting in His presence and listening to worship music. And then there were times He would be silent, and I would choose how I wanted to spend time with Him. As I entered into Bible readings, I would first invite Him into my time, asking Him to illuminate Scripture that He wanted me to meditate on. Then, I would reflect with Him on how to apply the truth of His written Word into my life.

Regardless of what I was doing during my devotional time, I intentionally engaged with God. He became my focus, not what I was doing. God was teaching me another element in how to move from a lifestyle of 'doing' to a mode of 'being'. Essentially, He was teaching me to abide: the practice of communing and worshiping Him with my spirit (John 4:23-24).

My relationship with God was enriched as I invited Him into my devotional space. I learned how to interact with Him as a friend. The concept of abiding became such a dynamic principle that I practiced and learned to abide continuously. Our devotional times became a two-way conversation and communion. At times, words were spoken between us, whereas there were other times our spirits communed without words. I experienced the verse: *"Pray continually."* (1 Thessalonians 5:17, NIV)

High Standard of Holy Living

As I began to hear God's voice more and more, He led me into a season of intense reading and learning. Holy Spirit drew me into the Bible and directed me to other books by Christian authors. During this time, God challenged me deeply.

Holy Spirit called me to give up bad attitudes and habits, and then He retrained me through the Living Word of the Bible into operating with godly thinking and with a godly lifestyle. This was a new level of refining. God would first reveal one area of my life that needed work. Next, I would submit to Him and His sanctification process, after which I would learn to implement what He wanted me to. Then, He would immediately work on the next area in my life that needed changing. This season was incredibly intense and intentional on God's part as He motivated me into a holy lifestyle that honoured Him.

As this intense sanctification process was happening, I began to look around at my biblical community. They were not experiencing what I was experiencing. Why were they not being refined as I was? Why do I alone have to be in

20

this radical season of change? I was quick to compare my journey to that of my friends and was tempted to mirror their journey and slow the intensity of my sanctification.

God spoke into my thoughts:

"Deanna, My journey with you is your journey alone. Do not slow your pace to match those around you. If you slow down, you will not move with the speed or into the direction that I desire for your life. Keep your eyes on My Spirit and move in step with My Spirit (Galatians 5:25). Then you will move into the fullness of life that I desire for you."

Desire and Passion

As I learned more about how to be in relationship with God, I experienced Holy Spirit stirring my heart for His hurting church. I was saddened that many Christians in my life were hurting physically, emotionally, and spiritually. Why did Christians overall not appear holistically healthier than non-Christians?

I began to search God and Scriptures related to healing. Did God heal today? I was not content with the simple, trite, church answers that I had heard in the past. If God is the same yesterday, today, and forever, then why were we not seeing miracles of healing today in the church? Like myself, I saw many friends struggling emotionally. I knew that there had to be freedom in Jesus Christ, for freedom is a promise given in Scripture (Galatians 5:1).

So many Christians are hurting in our church, Lord. My heart is grieved for them. I don't expect to understand what is going on spiritually or otherwise, but I would ask that You reveal what You want me to see and that You would give me the words to pray into people's lives. You continue to increase my passion, desires, emotions. My spirit is stirring, and I'm not sure what direction You are leading me. This passion is taking me quite off guard. I desire to minister and nurture, to shed the truth of Your Scripture into situations. Breathe on my giftings to help me to be effective in the areas that You desire me to serve.

Help me to hear Your voice and not be deceived. Show me where to be involved. I trust Your timing, and I trust Your will and Your way for me. Help me to be patient in waiting on You. I love You and adore You. Continue to move in my life and lead me in the direction that You want me to go.

<u>*Father God*</u>*: "My child, you are troubled about so many things. Take heart, for I have overcome the world. I will be with you, I will guide you, and I will take care of you. Lean on Me. Love me. You know that I will be faithful."*

In the midst of my questions, I somehow knew that the desires and passions within me were there to move me towards an area where I would eventually serve the Body of Christ.

Inner Healing, Deliverance, and Discipleship

As Holy Spirit worked in my heart, I heard about a ministry called Ellel Ministries that was based within my city. Ellel Ministries believes that Jesus is passionate about bringing healing and freedom. While He was on earth, Jesus cared about the physical, emotional, and spiritual needs of those who looked to Him for help and brought freedom, life, and wholeness wherever He went. Jesus has anointed His people to fulfill the same commission. The heart of the ministry of Ellel was similar to my heart in this season: to see Jesus restore His people, bring healing and transformation, and equip them to fulfill all the plans God has for them.

Harvey and I attended a weekend-long retreat called a "Healing Retreat" led by Ellel Ministries. At this retreat, we received teaching about root problems that may be the cause of a person's struggle: unforgiveness, personal sin, generational sin, wounding, or other strongholds of the enemy. We were led through a personal process of forgiveness, repenting, and making godly choices. Then, we prayed for the Lord to bring His healing and deliverance into our lives. Being led by Holy Spirit, the prayer ministers at the retreat used their learned tools to walk Harvey and me through our issues at a very personal level into a place of inner healing. After the retreat, I experienced an increased measure of freedom in my spiritual and emotional life.

That weekend was a significant part of my journey as the questions I had about healing and the abundant life in Jesus Christ were being answered. Harvey and I were so impacted by this ministry that we began training to learn more about the spiritual principles behind it so that we could minister inner healing, deliverance, and discipleship to other Christians. However, after I was trained and ready to minister to others, God clearly closed this door. Inner healing and deliverance ministry was not where He wanted me to serve.

I am "Too Much"

As I experienced more freedom in Jesus Christ through the biblical principles of Ellel, I readily shared the teaching and my experiences with my friends. At the time, I was leading a women's Bible study, and Harvey and I were leading a couples group. Some of my friends were happy for me. However, many of my friends were reluctant to readily receive what I had experienced as truth. I began to recognize that most of my friends were content to stay where they were at in their Christian walk, and they did not like hearing about my passions related to healing and the fullness of life that is accessible to Christians. My passions seemed to threaten their way of thinking as it related to Christianity. I began to feel that I was "too much" in my thinking, my passions, and my desires. In a desire to be accepted for who I was, I began to tone myself down and be selective as to whom I would talk to in relation to my newfound freedom in Jesus. Eventually, I began to receive acceptance from a few, selected friends who were like-minded in their passions and desires. Even though I was experiencing rejection from many of my Christian friends, the freedom that I was experiencing in my relationship with Jesus and Father God compelled me to continue to wholeheartedly journey with Holy Spirit.

Desiring the Gifts of Holy Spirit

My biblical discipline at this time in my life consisted of reading through the entire Bible. In my reading, I came across (1 Corinthians 12:7-11):

"A spiritual gift is given to each of us so we can help each other. To one person the Spirit gives the ability to give wise advice; to another the same Spirit gives a message of special knowledge. The same Spirit gives great faith to another, and to someone else the one Spirit gives the gift of healing. He gives one person the power to perform miracles, and another the ability to prophesy. He gives someone else the ability to discern whether a message is from the Spirit of God or from another spirit. Still another person is given the ability to speak in unknown languages, while another is given the ability to interpret what is being said. It is the one and only Spirit who distributes all these gifts. He alone decides which gift each person should have."

This list shocked me, as I had never read this list in isolation before. I had always learned about the gifts of Holy Spirit lumped in with teaching, evangelism, and other gifts listed in the Bible. I thought, *"If these gifts are given to the believers, why have I not seen most of these gifts in my church? What would my church look like if these gifts of Holy Spirit were evident and operating freely?"* My daily Bible reading was halted for days as I meditated on and pondered this list with Jesus. I personally called these the "wooey, wooey gifts". They were delightfully mysterious and supernatural to me.

25

Eventually my Bible reading continued on to the love chapter (1 Corinthians 13), and then I was hit with 1 Corinthians 14:1:

"Follow the way of love and eagerly desire gifts of the Spirit, especially prophecy." (NIV)

What? I was always taught that Holy Spirit dealt out the gifts like 1 Corinthians 12 says, and my part was to passively and thankfully receive whatever He decided to give me. This thought was new for me: desire on MY part could bring about these supernatural gifts? Yeah! I immediately reversed my logical, sequential, Bible reading and jumped back to 1 Corinthians 12. I began to pray and ask God for these gifts from Holy Spirit. But, how could I decide which gift to ask for? How could I choose just one? Since there were no restrictions on the number of gifts to ask for, I decided to ask for all of them, but I especially began to ask for the gift of prophecy. I had a few experiences of someone prophesying over me, and in those prophetic words, I had experienced the power of God. I wanted this gift! I desired to bless others in the way that I had experienced being supernaturally blessed through prophecy.

I was quick to share my excitement and new understanding of the gifts of Holy Spirit with my friends and the groups that I was leading. Again, I experienced a few who were happy for me, but most of them did not know what to do with me. With time, I realized that the people that I was leading were more interested in learning about the spiritual basics of Christianity: spiritual 'basketball' and spiritual 'volleyball'. I, however, was interested in learning about spiritual 'bungee jumping'! I naturally gravitated to the power and supernatural edge of God.

In my passion for Holy Spirit and His gifts, I naively assumed that all Christians would want to experience their life being transformed by Holy Spirit as I did. I quickly realized that most of my Christian friends were cautious and for the most part sceptical of my experiences. I realized that these individuals were hesitant because they did not want to change their view of God, their theology, or their Christian way of life. They had God in a nicely and neatly defined box, and they did not appreciate me poking at it.

Spiritual Bungee Jumpers

I continued leading these two groups, giving them what they desired (spiritual basics), but I began to ask God to send me other Christians with similar, spiritual yearnings. Within a short season, God sent three friends into my life that were as passionate as I was regarding spiritual gifts and living an abundant Christian life. They gravitated to me, and we journeyed together with Holy Spirit, sharing stories and delighting in each other's adventures! These ladies became my *"iron sharpens iron"* friends (Proverbs 27:17). How they chose to live their Christianity and their hunger for the Lord added fuel to my fire.

As I daily prayed and earnestly desired the gift of prophecy, God led me to read Graham Cooke's book, *Approaching the Heart of Prophecy*. I remember in the middle of reading his book, I thought, *"Why am I reading this book when I don't even have the gift of prophecy?"* God prompted me to continue because He knew this gift was coming from Holy Spirit. Slowly, my gift of prophecy revealed itself and grew as I began to practice prophesying in my small, safe community of friends.

The Great Sadness

In the fall of 2005, I was experiencing joy in my journey with Holy Spirit, but I recognized that I still struggled in emotionally connecting with my husband, children, and with Father God and Jesus. I did not realize it at the time, but the demonic spirit that had attached to my emotions as a child still had a hold on me.

Yet, God's hand of grace had been upon me for the past 15 years so that I could experience being who I was created to be and experience relationship with Him. In His strategic plan for my healing, He had systematically dismantled the wall that Satan had erected to keep me emotionally disconnected from Jesus. Holy Spirit had taught me what I needed to learn to be an overcomer. He had coached me in the following disciplines and principles:

- How to make worship a lifestyle
- How to be led by His Spirit
- How to hear His voice
- How to implement inner healing principles
- How to live out biblical principles for a holy life

Holy Spirit also led me to my small community of like-minded believers that purely loved me, supported my journey, and provided a safe environment to grow in the prophetic.

I was fully equipped for entering one of my most difficult seasons. God showed me that my healing and freedom journey was not over. He revealed to me that Satan still had a foothold on my emotions. In God's sovereignty, He removed His hand of grace upon this demonic foothold and allowed it to surface again in my emotions so that I could implement what He had taught me and walk out of this bondage into victory. His desire was for me to walk out the spiritual principle of Romans 16:19-20:

"...be wise about what is good, and innocent about what is evil. The God of peace will soon crush Satan under your feet..." (NIV)

This was my opportunity to become more than a conqueror (Romans 8:37) and crush Satan underneath <u>my</u> feet. Yet, as the demonic foothold was uncovered, I instantly stepped into a deep and dark depression that lasted for fifteen months. My passions and desires were suddenly gone, and I lost satisfaction in my responsibilities as a mom, a wife, and in leading my groups. My beautiful times of communion and relationship with the Lord seemed to grow cold and one-sided. I felt like I was doing all the talking, and God was mostly silent. I did not understand where this depression had come from as my life and spiritual rhythms had not changed. I was not doing anything differently.

I was forced to rely on God day-by-day. One thing I did recognize was that this depression felt strangely familiar. I articulated with my friends that I felt like I used to feel as a child. I could sense that there was a familiarity to this emotional oppression. As a child, I had simply accepted this emotional turmoil as a part of who I was because I had not known any differently. There was a drastic difference in this season as an adult experiencing this oppression once again. As this demonic foothold resurfaced, I *knew* that this emotional turmoil was <u>not</u> meant to be a part of my life. I *knew* that this harassment was from the enemy, and this time I was prepared to fight. And fight I did! I pushed harder into the Lord: I read my Bible more, read more devotional books, worshiped more, and listened more. And...nothing changed.

My natural tendency was to move back into 'doing' when I was hit with spiritual difficulty. I quickly learned that my ideas and efforts to walk into freedom were useless and powerless.

Journal Entry: December 2005

My tormented soul finds comfort from only You, and I cannot find You. Have You withdrawn from me? Why do You not comfort me? Have I displeased You? Why do You not speak to me? How long must I be in such anguish?

After months of trying to fight for my freedom on my own, I had an especially hopeless day and expressed my frustrations to Harvey. As he listened to all that I was doing to try and move out of the depression, he said, "Deanna, I think you are trying too hard." There was wisdom in what he said, so I decided to try a different approach. Spiritually, I dropped my entire 'doing' list. Instead, I chose to rest in the Lord, choosing to trust that if I needed to do something to move forward, He would show me.

I desperately wanted God to bring wholeness to my emotions, and it was so easy to make what He could do for me the focus instead of making relationship with Him the focus. Holy Spirit once again led me to choose to make loving God my first priority. My thoughts and my mind were my battlefield where Holy Spirit led me to take every thought captive to the obedience of Christ. I chose each day to make healthy, emotional decisions. Every day, I did something that I enjoyed (painting, dancing, reading), and I chose to surround myself with people that filled me and did not drain me.

During my depression, I was praying and seeking Holy Spirit's counsel on whether I should seek medical help. Holy Spirit clearly showed me that I was not to take medication. He knew that, for me, my depression was spiritually related and not a result of a chemical imbalance. He continued to lead me towards spiritual freedom.

Holy Spirit was faithful in showing me how I needed to cooperate with Him for me to receive my healing. While attending an Emotional Healing teaching at Ellel Ministries, Holy Spirit revealed that there were curses and pronouncements made over me as a child. Through personal, prayer ministry with prayer counsellors at Ellel, these pronouncements and curses were spiritually broken off of my life.

Journal Entry: December 2005

Thank you, Holy Spirit, for revealing the curses and pronouncements made over me by others and myself. You fought for me once again. I thank You.

You are showing me that true ministry flows out of a relationship with You and knowing You intimately. 'Doing' flows from 'being' with You. I am still so far from the mark. I think the biggest blessing You can give me is more of a desire for You, not what You can do or will do, just You. Show me how to just be with You.

So much of how I have lived is to 'do'. You are continuing to call me to 'be' and to be with You. My whole mindset has been to obey You and follow You so that You can use me. But is my focus all wrong? I am created for relationship with You. My doing simply flows from this. Help me to truly live each day. Help me to enjoy and commune with You. Forgive me for striving. Show me how to abide, rest, and be still. Show me how to live in and truly engage in each moment of the day.

<u>Father God</u>: "My Child, press into My heart. Blessings flow through you to your children. Hold fast to My truths, obey Me, and follow. Boldness, holiness. <u>Fear not!</u>"

God began to highlight multiple, spiritual roots that had helped to establish the grip of this demonic stronghold. Sometimes the roots were established through sin in my own life, and some roots were established by how I chose to respond to the sin of others against me. Holy Spirit would give me Scripture verses and show me when I needed to implement spiritual principles of repentance and forgiveness as He allowed these issues in my life to be revealed.

During this time, listening to Holy Spirit's voice and resting in the Lord became my main spiritual disciplines. Prayer, reading the Bible, submission, and obedience were also a part of my daily rhythm. Occasionally, I would revert to habitual and unhealthy ways of dealing with my emotions in my day-to-day life such as ignoring my emotions, isolating myself, or meeting my own emotional needs instead of relying on God. Through this process, I felt like I was not making progress. But with time, I could see that I was moving forward; the speed was just much slower than I would have liked. My momentum in my healing seemed to be: two steps forward, one step back, two steps forward, and one step back.

Loneliness

One of the most predominate feelings that I had in this season was loneliness. When I first felt the depression coming over me, I expressed my feelings of loneliness to God. He clearly asked me, *"Am I enough?"*

When He first spoke this, I thought that it was the end of my loneliness, but it was just the beginning. I had become too dependent on my friends to meet my emotional needs instead of going to God first. I was still involved in leading two Christian groups, and my life appeared to be surrounded by friends. But in this season, I found out who my true friends were. Some of my friends did not know how to deal with my emotional mess, so they did nothing. As a result, I realized how much I had been the one to take the initiative in my relationships, and when I could not take the initiative due to this dark season, most of my friends exited my life.

My spiritual community became very small. I was left with just my three, spiritual, bungee jumping friends. These friends accepted me where I was at, emotional mess and all. I could be real with them, and they would still love me. Sensitive to the voice of Holy Spirit and passionate about their walk with the Lord, they were a source of great encouragement to me and continued to support me in my relationship with the Lord.

Picture of Being in Jesus

In the spring of 2006, I was sensing and feeling that I had journeyed through the worst of the demonic stronghold on my emotions. I was not feeling depression harass me every day. At a deeper level, I was learning how to be and how to live the first commandment: loving the Lord my God with all my heart, soul, and strength (Deuteronomy 6:5). God gave me a beautiful picture of what it looks like to 'be' in Jesus (John 15:5), and then He showed me how 'doing' flows out of this.

Journal Entry: March 2006

One thing You have taught me is how to live and be in Jesus. I see a picture of myself with an invisible Jesus completely surrounding my body. As I see Him moving His arm, I follow and move my arm. I wait for His lead.

Jesus only did and said what He saw His Father doing (John 5:19). This is how Jesus did 'doing' in His life. His doing flowed out of knowing and being with His Father – out of relationship with Him. He did not act on His own ideas or His own initiative. As I live in Jesus and become sensitive to His heart and His movements in my relationship with Him, then, as He moves, I move. As He speaks, I speak. As I mimic Jesus' movements for my life as He follows Father's movements, then I will be in step with Father's will and desire for the destiny of my life!

Fire of Desire Stoked

As Holy Spirit led me out of depression, I began to feel once again. Passions for the gifts of Holy Spirit and the desire for Christians to be moving and living in the fullness of who they are in Jesus Christ began to be stirred at a deep level in my heart. God used the following verses to encourage me to approach His throne of grace with confidence and in intercession for His people and myself:

"Up to this time you have not asked a [single] thing in My Name [as presenting all that I AM]; but now ask and keep on asking and you will receive, so that your joy (gladness, delight) may be full and complete." (John 16:24, AMPCE)

"Streams of tears flow from my eyes because my people are destroyed. My eyes will flow down unceasingly, without relief, until the Lord looks down from heaven and sees." (Lamentations 3:48-50, NIV)

I continued to pray for my own healing and the healing of others in my life.

Gentle Deliverance

Through revelation from Holy Spirit, I became aware that this demonic spirit had attached to my emotions somewhere around the time that I was a toddler. I knew that the spirit had descended through my family line and had gained its foothold through sin that had somehow gained an entrance into my family generations back. The extended family members that I knew were all Christians. However, what was evident in my family line was a strong and persistent element of control and manipulation towards others. The only godly control that the Bible speaks about is self-control (Galatians 5:22-24). Holy Spirit does not try to control us. Instead, He releases freedom (2 Corinthians 3:17). As Holy Spirit operates in freedom and empowers us, so should we give freedom to others. Anytime someone tries to control another person or try to make him or her do something that they don't want to do, this is manipulation. It is not godly, and it is a sin. I began to suspect that this was the generational sin that had opened the door for the enemy to gain access to my family line.

I certainly did not have all the details of the 'how' and 'why' of the demonic stronghold, but as soon as I had a sense that there was a demonic spirit that had a hold on my emotions, I began to pray for deliverance. My girlfriends were trained in deliverance and began to pray for me and with me. I expected that this was how I would be delivered, but God had other plans.

Holy Spirit invited me to engage in a new spiritual discipline, that of praying in tongues. Holy Spirit led me to pray for roughly ten minutes every day for forty days. I had learned about praying in tongues through John Bevere's book, *Drawing Near*. After learning about this gift, I began to pray for it, and within a short time, I received the gift of tongues from Holy Spirit. On the first day of my forty days of prayer discipline, I saw a picture of myself:

Journal Entry: August 2006

Holy Spirit gave me a vision today of myself. I feel that it is a picture of how I currently am. I was a gray watercolor painting. As I prayed in tongues, it began to gently rain on me. As the rain fell on my head, it caused the gray to run and slowly wash off of me.

I sense that the gray represents the demonic stronghold that is on my emotions. As it washes off of me, I can see that my healed and delivered self is underneath, and I am bright, colorful, and beautiful.

I was very encouraged by this vision. As the forty days progressed, God brought this vision back to me on more than one occasion, and I realized that, bit-by-bit, this demonic foothold was gently being washed away. I was being delivered! I knew by the end of the forty days that God had completely delivered me from this demonic foothold that had had a grip on me for 37 years!

Emotionally Healed

As I began to live in the fullness of my emotional healing, questions remained buried in my mind that I could not ask God about because I felt they threatened what I knew of His character and goodness. Deep inside, I wanted to know why God had allowed the demonic spirit to manifest, and why He had allowed the depression to last for 15 months. These experiences had been so hard and tormenting. How could a good God who loved me allow this to happen? Deliverance was so easy for Him. Why had He not just delivered me at the beginning of my journey?

I received my answer while attending a teaching session at Ellel Ministries. They taught that God desires for us to live in continued freedom once He delivers us from any foothold of Satan in our lives. God knew that I needed to grow in my relationship with Him to stay free. It was vital that I learn to trust Him and to rest in Him and not work my way toward spiritual maturity on my own. Call this discipleship or call it a maturing process, but God knew the requirements that were essential to hold the ground He was giving me. Thus, the *journey* and *process* of healing was necessary.

Yes, deliverance was and is easy for God. However, I had learned so many bad habits over the decades in trying to cope with this demonic foothold on my emotions, and they required time and retraining to undo. The process was long because I needed to be taught how to hold the spiritual ground once I was delivered. In addition, I had to practice living with the expanse of the emotions that God gave my personality through my healing and learn how to steward these emotions correctly. Holy Spirit showed me that He very personally had mentored me in this learning process, and I basked in the revelation of God's goodness towards me. He knew exactly how my emotional healing journey needed to look like. I could clearly see that now.

The key to my emotional healing was not about following a formula. My emotional healing came because of, first and foremost, learning how to love the Lord my God and connecting with all members of the Holy Trinity. Then, Holy Spirit very personally led me step-by-step into my personal healing and victory. I was living in the promise of Jesus giving me *"beauty for ashes, the oil of joy for mourning, the garment of praise for the spirit of heaviness."*[1] I emerged from my dark season with praise on my lips! The thankfulness I felt for the price that Jesus had paid for me to step into emotional freedom was beyond what I could express in words. I was also delighted to continue to discover afresh who God had created me to be!

Shortly after my emotional healing, Holy Spirit asked me to stop leading both Bible study groups. My spiritual community now consisted of my three, spiritual, bungee jumping friends.

---

[1] (Isaiah 61:3, NKJV)

Emotional Restoration

Our God is a God of restoration. Where Satan has killed, stolen from us, or destroyed parts of our life, God desires to restore it.

"So I will restore to you the years that the swarming locust has eaten..." (Joel 2:25a, NKJV)

What I love about God's heart is that He does not just restore what the enemy has originally stolen, He restores through multiplication. Look at the story of Job. God increased and multiplied (doubled) what was taken from him (Job 42:10). And, multiplication in restoration is also found in Isaiah:

"Instead of shame and dishonor, you will enjoy a double share of honor. You will possess a double portion of prosperity in your land, and everlasting joy will be yours." (Isaiah 61:7, emphasis mine)

This is the goodness of God in full effect! This is His vengeance on Satan – to give back to us even more than what was originally taken from us. This was the basis of my prayers for restoration in my life. I had over thirty years of living as a shadow of who I was created to be. Once I started to live as God intended without the emotional oppression of the enemy, I recognized that there were areas of my emotions that needed a restorative touch from the Lord. I began to pray that the fullness of that restoration would hold a double portion of God's original plan.

As I continued to practice what Holy Spirit had taught me about engaging in relationship with the Holy Trinity, I rarely felt afraid any more to be known intimately by

Father God. The 'being' was becoming easier and more natural to me. Restoration was coming in a measure, but I still could not feel a connection of love with Jesus or Father God. Regardless of how I was feeling, I continued to interact with God in faith with my mind and with my will.

Increase in My Prophetic Gift

An area where I saw almost instant restoration in was my ability to hear God's voice and in my gift of prophecy. This gift that I had desired for years and had experienced occasionally, began to show up in a new strength as I listened to God for myself and for others. A predominate way that Holy Spirit speaks to me is through visions and impressions. My visions increased, and I also began to hear and receive information from Holy Spirit in a variety of different ways.

As Holy Spirit began to fully awaken my ability to engage with Him, I was drawn into an even deeper relationship with Him. I remember one particular, quiet time where Holy Spirit brought to my remembrance things that I had previously prayed for. It dawned on me that Holy Spirit was leading me into living the promises in the Bible – my personal 'Promised Land' – a land "*flowing with milk and honey*."[2] This was a precious time with Holy Spirit.

I consciously continued to abide and engage with Holy Spirit as I went through the rest of my day. As I was shopping later, a Starbucks caught my eye, and I immediately heard Holy Spirit say, "*Come have coffee with Me.*" I chose to be flexible, let go of my 'to do' list, and act on what I sensed Holy Spirit saying. I walked into the

---

[2] (Leviticus 20:24)

Starbucks and saw the feature drink: Honey Latte. Yup –
milk and honey! I had a good chuckle with Holy Spirit,
enjoyed my honey latte with Him, and sensed His pleasure
with me in that intimate moment.

I began to live in the adventure of the verse:

*"It is God's privilege to conceal things and the king's
privilege to discover them."* (Proverbs 25:2)

When I would sense Holy Spirit saying something to me,
I would intentionally interact with Him, act on it, and then
see what He would say or do next. At times, the adventures
were like the Honey Latte adventure, and Holy Spirit would
affirm, "*You're hearing me, girl!*" On other occasions, Holy
Spirit would lead me into very deep places, and He would
teach me truths about God and the Bible. Some adventures
were short, and I would immediately see its end as I acted
on His prompting. Other times, the adventure would last
months.

As I journeyed and adventured with Holy Spirit, I
experienced a greater depth of life, freedom, and joy that I
had never experienced in my Christian walk before. His
fruit was unmistakeable as I was learning to continuously
abide.

As I began to know and love Holy Spirit deeper, He
began to give me other gifts. I quickly realized how
supernatural Holy Spirit was when He began to give me
supernatural experiences and angelic encounters. I was so
thankful to have my safe, loving, biblical community to talk
to about my experiences and help align them with biblical
principles.

Holy Spirit began to do immeasurably more than I could
ask or imagine in my life and within my small community.
I never realized before just how much fun and what an

adventure Christianity could be! I certainly did not expect to experience supernatural events just by engaging with Holy Spirit and learning to hear His voice, but I began to understand that listening to God is, in fact, a supernatural activity. And as you engage with Him in a supernatural way, He often opens up and delivers more than you expected.

As I was communing with Holy Spirit, He continued to drastically transform me. As this transformation took place, it was vital that I was a part of a community of like-minded believers. My small, spiritual, bungee jumping community was a safe place for me to be vulnerable, share, and to risk trying out my spiritual gifts. God created the Body of Christ for a reason, and I honestly believe that my relationship with Holy Spirit would not have been as rich or as deep had I journeyed with Holy Spirit alone.

A friend once said to me, "The ways of Holy Spirit are better caught than taught." I believe this statement is true. I believe that learning to know Holy Spirit, His ways, and using His gifts takes time. Learning about Holy Spirit occurs as I deliberately pursue Him in relationship, share my experiences with others, and celebrate what He is teaching me. As others also share, their learning becomes my learning, their hunger for God fuels my hunger, and iron sharpens iron.

As difficult as parts of my spiritual journey was, I can see repeatedly how God had His faithful, loving fingerprints on my life. God blessed me with my parents, husband, and strategic Christians to provide me with the support that I needed to discover my healing and walk into wholeness. My biblical community was established, my emotional healing was in process, and exploring my identity and discovering my destiny awaited me.

Elements

Original painting by Deanna Oelke

Again Jesus said, "Peace be with you! As the Father has sent me, I am sending you." And with that he breathed on them and said, "Receive the Holy Spirit." (John 20:21-22, NIV)

I painted this picture for the first time during worship at a conference. I called it "Wind of Holy Spirit" and just included the wind. Painting it the second time in my studio, I wanted to capture different aspects and elements of Holy Spirit that the worship dancer is experiencing: wind of Holy Spirit (Acts 2:1-2), fire of God (Hebrews 12:29), and the water of life (Revelation 22:17). Jesus is also represented by the Rose of Sharon in the wind.

Chapter 2

My Journey into Identity and Destiny

New Vision and Hope for the Future

In the spring of 2007, God used a negative situation to act as a catalyst in my life. Specifically, He opened my eyes to see His vision of what the gift of prophecy could look like within the Body of Christ.

My long-term, career plan was to return to teaching once my children were both in school full-time. With this plan in mind, I began applying for teaching jobs. Now, I was an excellent teacher with a good history throughout my teaching career. Therefore, I fully expected to be welcomed with open arms into a school. However, this did not happen. Instead, I was turned down for all the jobs that I applied to.

As the summer commenced, I realized that I would not be returning to my teaching career in the fall. I was jobless and feeling hopeless. If I did not return to teaching as my career, what would I do? When my children went to school in the fall, I would have a whole lot of time on my hands...and this thought terrified me. All the reteaching that God had done in my life to date regarding my identity being found in my relationship with the Lord and not in what I do would now be put into practice.

Again, Holy Spirit used this opportunity to take me deeper into the heart of Father God. In addition, He brought me to a greater understanding of myself so that I could comprehend what He was showing me and then cooperate with Him to make the necessary changes. I am so thankful that Holy Spirit first worked on my relationship with Him and with Father God. I had learned to trust them both, and trust was what I needed as Holy Spirit revealed sins, false comforts, and false self-protection.

Journal Entry: July 1, 2007

How is it possible to feel pain, rejection, disappointment, and hopelessness for the future all in one swoop? The only hope that I have for the future is hope in the Lord, and I don't know how to do this, Jesus! I am so hurt, so disillusioned. I come before You empty-handed, desiring to be faithful...feeling that I could stray so easily. I will follow Your lead.

In this season, You are teaching me:

- *How to make You first when I see no plans for my future*
- *How to continue to worship You in this place*

False comforts/self-protection:

- *I push others away to accomplish my tasks. My tasks and my ministry become my priority over my relationship with people and my family.*
- *I choose not to hope so that I won't be disappointed when it does not happen.*

"Father, I sense You are calling me to hope in the plans that You have for me, plans that will prosper me and not harm me (Jeremiah 29:11), and to hope in Your goodness – that I will see the goodness of the Lord in the land of the living (Psalm 27:13). I don't want to dream and risk again. I don't want to experience more broken dreams, more hope dying. I want to give up. I believe that You are not good – and I know that this is a lie! You are a good, good Father (Psalm 100:5). Show me how to love You in this place and how to risk again. I have to believe that my world will get better than this."

I had placed my hope for the future in my teaching career continuing. My future, in my mind, was certain and guaranteed. When teaching was taken away, I suddenly realized how uncertain my future really was. I experienced such fear and vulnerability. I had to embrace hope in the Lord and choose to trust in His faithfulness in the midst of my uncertain future. Regardless of what my future held, I needed to rely fully on Him to lead me. There was a

47

renewing of my mind that was required. I wanted my heart to believe what the Psalmist declared:

"We put our hope in the Lord.
He is our help and our shield.
In him our hearts rejoice,
for we trust in his holy name.
Let your unfailing love surround us, Lord,
for our hope is in you alone." (Psalm 33:20-22)

Within this difficult place of seeing a need for restoration, Father spoke to me so clearly and tenderly:

"Deanna, express your love to Me in new ways. I will show you how to love Me without reservation, limitations, or control. Holy, I will make you holy. Love Me."

Again, He was calling me into the first and greatest commandment: to love the Lord my God with all my heart, soul, mind, and strength (Mark 12:29-30). He was simplifying my seemingly ambiguous journey of hoping in the Lord. All I had to do was respond to Him and commune with Him.

What I did not expect in moving forward was feeling waves of strong emotions. Many times, raw and uncomfortable emotions bubbled to the surface spontaneously within my day. Father, Jesus, and Holy Spirit were calling me in those moments to be real with my feelings and feel them in their presence, in safe places, and during pockets of time throughout the day. I cried every day for over a month.

I realized after a few weeks of daily weeping that one of the feelings that I was feeling was grief. I was grieving the lost hope for my future and the possible death of my

48

teaching career. Naming my feelings as well as feeling them in the presence of Jesus helped me to immerse myself in the process of healing to the depth that Holy Spirit desired. In the midst of the grieving, my fear of the future, and hopelessness, Holy Spirit continued to encourage me.

Journal Entry: July 24, 2007

"So be strong and courageous. Do not be afraid and do not panic before them. For the Lord your God will personally go ahead of you. He will neither fail you nor abandon you." (Deuteronomy 31:6)

"They will be my people, and I will be their God. I will give them singleness of heart and action, so that they will always fear me and that all will then go well for them and for their children after them. I will make an everlasting covenant with them: I will never stop doing good to them, and I will inspire them to fear me, so that they will never turn away from me. I will rejoice in doing them good and will assuredly plant them in this land with all my heart and soul." (Jeremiah 32:38-41, NIV)

Father God: "Deanna, I want you to grow deeper and deeper in love with Me. It will be grander than anything you can imagine! I am so, so big, and I want to take you into My bigness. You will be surprised by what you find!"

I so desperately wanted this singleness of heart! Yet, I felt that my heart was divided and prone to idolatry. I earnestly desired that my children would inherit a godly fear of the Lord, would whole-heartedly love God, and would never turn away from Him. But I was again feeling that I could not connect my heart to the heart of Father God. I could neither feel love for Him nor could I feel God's love for me.

My personal healing and leaving a godly legacy for my children gave me the vision and motivation that I needed to continue moving forward. I needed to journey through my pain and choose, by faith, to believe that wholeness and restoration was God's intention for me. I knew that numbing the pain and choosing to not feel the emotions as they bubbled to the surface would lead me into the bondage of depression. Experience had taught me that I could not numb only my painful emotions. Numbing some of them would lead to numbing all of them, including happiness, joy, and contentment. I determined not to go down this formerly well-trodden path of depression. The alternative was to forge a new path: to journey daily through the pain, trusting that Jesus would restore me, and choosing to believe that this mourning would only last for a time and not be forever (Psalm 30:5b).

My spiritual disciplines over the summer included:

- Reading the Bible
- Regular worship
- Feeling my feelings in the presence of Jesus
- Expressing my feelings to Jesus by speaking them out to Him in prayer or by journaling
- Listening to Holy Spirit's voice and asking how He was praying for me (Romans 8:26)
- Choosing to be vulnerable by sharing and crying with my biblical community who loved me

This was a difficult season and another intense period of refining. But the one characteristic of God that I continuously experienced was His unconditional love. When I was at my worst, He remained at His best. His voice especially was precious to me during this time.

Prophetic Haircutting Experience

As the summer ended, my anxiety and fear increased. I had yet to arrange or secure any plans for my time, and the thought of being left with 6 hours a day of free time scared me. My trust and hope in the Lord was put to the test.

Within the first week of school, I went to a new hairdresser that had been recommended to me by a stranger in a shopping mall. Very random, I know. Once I met the hairdresser, Mitchel, I quickly learned that he was not only a Christian but also operated in the gift of prophecy. The Lord knew that I needed to be blessed by someone in the Body of Christ through the gift of prophecy.

Journal Entry: September 6, 2007

I had my hair cut by Mitchel today. Wow! Thank you for Your faithfulness, Lord Jesus. This was his prophecy to me:

"I see you speaking in front of large groups of women. You will write many books. You will be traveling a lot. You will have a team of intercessors. Prayer and fasting is part of your preparation."

Throughout my haircut, God, You were showing me that You are still leading me and that You love me. Thanks, Lord. Thank you for giving me the hope to continue to press into You and press on into my future. You have blessed me with contentment and

*self-love. I needed the Body of Christ today; I couldn't
have got here on my own.*

There were some important truths that God wanted me
to embrace from this prophetic haircutting experience. In
this difficult and emotional place, I had felt so broken and
unlovely. Yet, I was worthy to receive the love of Father
God and the love of others. I had a place of belonging in the
Body of Christ even while I was a mess. Secondly, God was
showing me that He had a plan for me! Even if I didn't
have a vision, He certainly did. And He graciously gave me
a peek into that vision: speaking, writing, and traveling.
Even though I could not yet see how this was possible, God
could. Finally, He wanted to encourage me to dream once
again. Furthermore, I needed to expand my dreams to
embrace a future that was not necessarily confined to the
limits of traditional teaching because He could do
immeasurably more than I could ask or imagine
(Ephesians 3:20).

Prophetic Conference

A few weeks later, I had the opportunity to go to a
prophetic conference in Washington State where Shawn
Bolz and Larry Randolph were the prophetic speakers. I
had never heard either of these men before, and I had never
been to a prophetic conference. Before I left, Holy Spirit
gave me this verse:

*"Those who plant in tears will harvest with shouts of
joy. They weep as they go to plant their seed, but they
sing as they return with the harvest."*
(Psalm 126:5-6)

This verse hit me hard, especially as I was still weeping often during the day while I endeavoured to learn and practice how to place my hope in the Lord. Instead of believing that this was what the Lord wanted to do on this trip, I chose to ignore this verse. I did not dare hope that I could experience joy in this season.

On the long drive out to the conference with my good girlfriend, we shared deeply, prayed for each other, and ministered to each other. Once arriving at the beach house that we had rented, we were welcomed with open arms by four other girlfriends. These other friends had arrived at the beach house earlier and had already spent time shopping prior to our arrival. During their shopping trip, they had bought blouses on sale, finding one for each of us, sizes all perfect. The blouses were bright, colourful, flowery, full of ruffles, and, quite frankly, not at all my style. I politely said, "Thank you," and tucked it away in my suitcase, planning to never wear it.

The next day, we were all very excited as we drove to the first session of the conference. I was fervently praying that each one of us would be called out of the crowd and given a prophetic word from Shawn or Larry. My heart yearned for this touch from Holy Spirit.

Prophetic Word of Destiny

In the first session, Shawn shared some of his journey. I was so impacted by the level of radical abandon of love for Father God in which he lived his life. If I thought I was passionate in my ideas and had dreams about what life could be like in the fullness of Jesus Christ, it was nothing compared to Shawn's. I was challenged and inspired once again to live in full abandon according to who I was created to be within the fullness of Jesus Christ.

At the end of his teaching, he began to press into the Lord and ask Holy Spirit for people to prophecy to in the crowd. God in His kindness highlighted me out of the crowd, and Shawn delivered this prophetic word to me:

"I see this incredible, inspirational gift on you...and just the way you think is so unique. And so, as you have misunderstood your own personality and the way you think – because you have wondered about your gift mix – you haven't totally understood yourself. But hear! You are going to help people understand their gift mix. You're going to help people understand who they are. You're going to help them to live a better quality of life. I feel like you have keys to unlock life: Christian living to people. You have keys that are books and are manuals.

"I feel like you have a teaching, inspirational gift. God's been for years calling you. It's almost like you could have been a secular psychologist or counsellor...but that's not your calling. Your calling is to bring people into the highest quality of what they are to be doing and living. God has not only given you keys to unlock this, and tools, and your wonderful teaching gift, but it's what has trained you, yourself, and your own heart and your own life. And you're going to be able to give away very personally, and I want to encourage you to share your weakness. Share your journey of strength and weakness. It feels like you already are very vulnerable with people, and that is beautiful.

"I also want to encourage you to stay in a place where you are helping to focus people on the quality of life

that God wants them to live as opposed to the inner healing side even though you have it, and it is strong. You can always do inner healing, but I want to encourage you – the Lord wants to release a worldwide, teaching ministry through your life. And I believe that it is so strong, but I feel like if you stayed in the inner healing or just the counsel side, you will never touch the greater, which is the worldwide.

"But also, I believe that you are a secret missile to seeker-friendly churches, that your materials will even go to seeker-sensitive and to culturally irrelevant churches, usually to the prophetic-type mantle that is on someone like you. But you are going to be able to go in because the language you use is meant for all the way across the board of churches. It's going to go all the way across. You have this radical edge to you that you can go all the way across the church board.

"I'm prophesying huge because you've been carrying this, but you haven't let it all come up here yet [your mind], because it's so big you haven't really believed for the fullness of it. But I'm telling you, God has been allowing you to contend in your own self – your own personality, your own life – so that you can come to a place of full belief for this. And that's where you have been coming to, and a huge expanse in your mind just happened in the last few months. And it is time, not 10 years from now, it's time to take steps, and take steps, and take steps.

"So, we bless you today in the name of Jesus."

When I first heard my word from Shawn Bolz, I instantly felt the fruit of peace and hope. God affirmed that this word was indeed from Him by having information in the word that I recognized as truth and fact. Shawn spoke about: my inspirational gift, my teaching gift, how I teach out of my experiences and am vulnerable, and that I have inner healing training. These were pieces of information spoken forth of which there was no way Shawn could have known about unless God had told him.

As I reflected on this prophetic word, the main essence of the word gripped my heart:

"You are going to help people understand their gift mix...You're going to help them to live a better quality of life...Your calling is to bring people into the highest quality of what they are to be doing and living."

As soon as he said this, I knew in my spirit that this was true. This was (and is) exactly what I love to do with people! I had never been able to articulate it before, but this was it! I deeply desired this prophetic word to be manifested in my life. Therefore, I began to fervently pray for Holy Spirit to lead me in this direction that He wanted me to go.

An interesting part of the prophetic word came right at the very end:

"And it's time, not 10 years from now, it's time to take steps, and take steps, and take steps."

What was interesting about this part was that, whenever anyone would give me a visionary, prophetic word like this one, I would mentally and emotionally push it away, saying to myself, *"Yes, maybe ten years from now."* This was a way for me to not become too hopeful in my future and risk disappointment. Even as I was listening to Shawn's word, I was defaulting to the thinking, *"Maybe ten years from now."* Yet, God spoke directly into my thoughts in that moment, encouraging me to press into Him about my future and to dream, risk, and hope once again.

There were so many things in this prophetic word that were far larger than me, and I knew they could not be accomplished without the intervention of God in my life. Could I dare to hope that the fullness of this could come to pass? It still felt like something that was very far off into the future. Then, there was the mention of books. What would I even write about? Through this prophetic word, God was telling me, *"Dream bigger, darling! I have grand plans for you!"* There was still so much mystery and unknowns about my future, but now I had a clearer vision of what my future *could* hold. I was excited to journey with God to discover and unfold the details!

Prophetic Blessing of Identity

In the morning of the last day of the conference, I pulled my classy, black clothes out of the suitcase to wear for the day. Before I had a chance to change into my black clothes, I heard the Lord say, *"Wear the bright, flowered blouse that your friends bought for you."* I quickly responded, *"Uh...no, Lord."* But God was insistent, so eventually I submitted.

God revealed that the blouse was symbolic of something. However, as I put it on and looked in the mirror, I mentally and physically cringed. It was too flowery, had too many ruffles, was too colourful, and was too bold...just overall, too much! I quickly rummaged through my suitcase to find my jean jacket to wear over the blouse, attempting to tone it down. As soon as I put on my jean jacket, I felt reasonably satisfied. My blouse looked much calmer now and more acceptable in my eyes. Immediately, the Lord clearly spoke to me:

"This is exactly what you do with your personality. You feel like your personality is 'too much' for people, and you try to calm down your personality so that you will be accepted by others and fit in."

I immediately was impacted with the truth of this statement. Driving to the conference, I sat at the back of the van and let my tears flow. During worship at the church, I was overcome and knelt before the Lord, weeping and praying. Holy Spirit ministered into years and years of hurt, including the hurt of being misunderstood by people. When I had been my bold, passionate self in the past, I had experienced rejection regularly. These events commun- icated to me that I was "too much" for the community at large.

I had so desperately wanted to fit into social situations and the Body of Christ in general that I had chosen to water down my personality and stop expressing myself so that I would be accepted. In doing this, I had shrunk back from who God desired me to be. I had allowed the thoughts and words of others towards me shape my identity instead of going to Father God to gain His perspective about my identity. I had also gone to people to meet my emotional needs, and when these needs could not be met, I would choose to think, again, that I was "too much". My response would be to withdraw and meet my emotional needs myself.

As I lingered in God's presence, feeling my desperate need for my emotional needs to be met and my identity to be affirmed, I postured myself to receive from Him. In my deep places of need, loss, and grief, Father God spoke:

"Deanna, your emotional needs have been too great for any human to meet. Your past, present, and future emotional needs are not too large for Me to fill!"

Then, in vision, I saw my Heavenly Father filling me with living water (John 4:10). He filled me to overflowing...and He had more than enough to meet my needs.

After worship that day, I sat down ready to listen to Larry Randolph. It was cold in the church, so I was ready to put my jean jacket on over my bold, flowery blouse. Holy Spirit insisted that I keep the jacket off so that my blouse could be seen. Apparently, the Lord's symbolism was not done.

Larry shared a teaching on how to use words of knowledge and prophetic words and turn them into prophetic blessings. He then intended to model how to do this by pulling people out of the crowd and giving them prophetic blessings. I was sitting back in my seat quite comfortably thinking, *"Great! This is my time to watch others receive a word; I already got mine."* The next thing I knew, Larry pointed in my direction and said, "I want to bless you!" I looked around at my friends, thinking he was pointing at one of them. "Yes, I am pointing at you!" Me?? "Yes, stand up! That's how we do it in church." So, I stood. My bold, loud, bright, flowery, ruffled blouse again a symbol of my personality: bold, loud, bright, beautiful, and feminine. And with my blouse and my personality on display for all to see, this blessing was spoken over me:

"I just want to bless you. I want to speak a Father's blessing over your life, and I want to tell you something that is very blessing-filled for you. You have a hunger for the things of God, for the Word of God, and the supernatural power of God. So, there is

a cry in your heart as a daughter to see the supernatural expressed through your own life. You always have had a propensity and leaning towards healings and miracles, things that are extraordinary, things that push. But also, there is an equal thing in you about understanding the revelatory, and dream interpretation, and visions, and that sort of thing. So, there has been a war of supernatural desires in your heart.

"So as a prophetic father, I want to say simply to you: you do not have to choose between the two. I believe that God is going to give you a double measure – a double portion of that which your heart desires – because, daughter, what you desire is what God has put in your heart. You would not have desired it if God had not put it in your heart.

"So, I want you to get ready this next year. I want you to get ready for God to begin to express to you and to release to you some of the tools that are needed to build and bring forth some of the desires of your heart. It's your year of accelerated push, it's your year of going forward, and it's your year of breaking free from the gravitational pull of limitations that have held you back from becoming what you are called to be. So, get ready for extraordinary encounters with your destiny in the months and years to come, and get ready for God to open up the revelatory to you.

"So, we want to bless Deanna, and we want to say to her, "Be blessed." We give you a Father's blessing. We give you a Jacob's blessing. We bless you coming in, we bless you going out, we bless the works of your

hands, we bless you in the city, we bless you in the field, we bless what you're doing, we bless your past, and we bless your future. And we say – blessing on top of blessing is going to overtake you and overrun you, Deanna, in Jesus' name. So, Lord, we bless Deanna. Amen.

"I know some stuff about you that the Lord is doing that is incredible. You just have to rest assured in your heart that God is working everything out that concerns you. You are going to find God's blessing in a great and wonderful way.

"So, Lord, we bless her, and thank you for that. Thank you for the anointing that's in her life."

Larry was so accurate in his prophetic word. He had perfectly expressed the desires of my heart! To hear that these desires were not selfish or "too much" but were desires that Father had given me left me wowed! This just added fuel to the fire of my desire to ask for more of God and His good gifts. I sat down, overcome with emotion over God's goodness towards me.

As my personality and identity was unfurled in the purity of who God created me to be, God continued to reveal that the desires of my heart were gifts from Holy Spirit that He wanted to give to me. And it was as my identity and my gifts were paired together that I saw Father God smile, point to me, and say, *"Just right."* God's voice instantly silenced the negative feelings and voices from my past that had been communicating that I was "too much".

Sheaves of Joy

The next morning, I woke up at five o'clock. I lay on my back reflecting on the past five days. As I communed with Jesus, I had this unfamiliar feeling that I was eventually able to articulate. For the first time in my life, I was feeling emotionally and spiritually content! Tears of thankfulness and joy ran down my face. God reminded me of the verse He had highlighted to me right before coming out to the conference:

"Those who plant in tears will harvest with shouts of joy. They weep as they go to plant their seed, but they sing as they return with the harvest." (Psalm 126:5-6)

Instantly, in vision, I saw that my outstretched arms were full of sheaves of joy too large for me to carry!

Conference Reflections

As I shared my prophetic words with other prophetic friends, they were excited, and they celebrated with me the plans that God had for my future. The real test for me was to share this word with my husband, Harvey. Harvey had released and blessed me in my prophetic journey, but at this point, he was not journeying in it himself. He was what I call "prophetically curious". This gift of prophecy was new to him, so he chose to watch my journey and assess my gift by the fruit that he saw in my life.

When I showed him the video clip of the prophetic word, his response was, "Wow! There is no way that Shawn and Larry could have known personal details about you unless God showed them. As for the details about your future, I guess we will have to wait and see." He recognized that

God was in the prophetic word but still held the word loosely. Wisely, Harvey took the posture of 'let's see what happens and how God leads'. He wanted to wait to see if good fruit would grow from this prophetic word. If this word was from the Lord, then we would see God's hand leading us, and we would experience this prophetic word coming to pass in my life.

The prophetic word from Shawn given at the conference was a visionary word that spoke of possibilities for my future.

"I feel like you have keys to unlock life: Christian living to people. You have keys that are books and are manuals...your materials will even go to seeker-sensitive and to culturally irrelevant churches, usually to the prophetic-type mantle that is on someone like you. But you are going to be able to go in because the language you use is meant for all the way across the board of churches."

"I want to encourage you – the Lord wants to release a worldwide, teaching ministry through your life."

These two points appealed to how I was created – to have a large impact on the world. I certainly did not have a clear picture of what my ministry would look like and especially could not see what I could write about. Yet, God had a vision even if I could not see it. After receiving this word, I would frequently pull it out of my journal, reread it, and pray about it.

This prophetic word was so far into the future that I could not even see what the next steps were until they were right in front of me. The only thing I knew was that there was a possible future related to ministry in store for me.

This was a *huge* journey of faith where I was challenged to literally take the steps one at a time as I saw them, and they were revealed to me.

This was not just my journey, as this became Harvey's as well. Just prior to coming out to the conference, Harvey changed jobs and received a significant increase in his pay. God had orchestrated events financially so that I did not have to go back to work. We could afford for me to pursue the avenue of ministry and see where God led.

God gave me a taste at this conference of how He desired to lavish His love on me and meet my needs. God was more than willing and able to do this for me. What I needed to learn, and it would be difficult, was how to stay in an open, spiritual posture to receive from Father God. I had met my emotional needs on my own for over 37 years. There were multiple, unhealthy habits that I could so easily gravitate to. Part of Shawn's prophetic word to me was that my calling is to *"bring people into the highest quality of what they are to be living and doing."* Before I could teach others, God needed to teach me how to do this for myself.

I needed to learn how to come into the highest quality of LIVING:

- Contentment – I had to continue to practice living the first commandment: loving the Lord my God with all my heart, soul, and strength. It would be necessary to learn how to be content with God and God alone. In addition, I needed to be content with 'being' not 'doing'.
- Identity – It would be critical to have my mind continually renewed in who I was in Jesus Christ and in who I was created to be.
- Restoration – I needed to continue to pursue emotional and spiritual restoration until I was

completely restored. No matter how painful the process, I had to be determined to press on until restoration was complete.

I needed to learn how to come into the highest quality of DOING:

- Destiny – The Bible says, *"Your eyes saw my unformed body; all the days ordained for me were written in your book before one of them came to be."* (Psalm 139:16, NIV) I have a destiny that only I can complete – something to do in this life that only I can do. Part of the adventure is journeying with Holy Spirit to discover how my experiences, spiritual gifts, passions, abilities, and personality all work together to reveal my destiny.

For me, I knew my destiny was linked with ministry of some kind. However, God showed me that, in the past, I had made ministry an idol and had placed it above my love for Him and above my family. I could not afford this happening again. Instead, my ministry should flow out of the strength of my relationship with God. Furthermore, serving and being present for my family needed to come above ministry.

After this conference, my personal battle in moving into the fullness of who I was created to be and what I was created to do was just beginning. God in His kindness had given me a taste at the conference and a vision of what I was fighting for. He confirmed to me:

"You are on the right track, girl! Keep moving forward; keep fighting! The end will be worth it! You

will see the goodness of the Lord in the land of the living!"[3]

Moving forward with this perspective, I was determined to passionately pursue God.

Loving Prophetic Community

There was another aspect of this conference experience that I desired to explore. The teaching at the conference had personally impacted me, but there was also a huge impact on the group of friends that I went with. Our girlfriend time in between the conference sessions was filled with fun, sharing our hearts with each other, celebrating each other's journey, and deliberately loving each other. We chose to speak encouraging words to each other – calling out the beauty that we could naturally see within each other and also the external beauty that we saw. As we sensed that God wanted to speak through us prophetically, we obeyed, risked, and spoke what we believed He wanted to say. Daily, we received prophetic words for each other. We all experienced being lavished on and loved by Father God and being loved by each other. At the end of the conference five days later, we were all dramatically and supernaturally transformed.

We had experienced prophetic community at its best: women loving God and loving each other through the gift of prophecy. Through this wonderfully blessed time together, God gave me a snapshot of what the Body of Christ could look like when the gift of prophecy is embraced and freely used. The results were beautiful, dramatic, and supernatural. I now understood why Paul said in his letter

---

[3] (Psalm 27:13)

to the Corinthians, *"...I wish you could all prophesy..."* (1 Corinthians 14:5)

This was encouragement that impacted us all at a spirit level with supernatural results. Recognizing the importance of what we had experienced together, I knew I needed to find a community of believers in my home city that freely used the gift of prophecy. Could I find one?

The Prophetic Void

Returning home, my girlfriends and I were on a mission: to find a church in our city where the gift of prophecy was embraced and utilized regularly. We traveled to various churches and prophetic conferences within our city. After months of field trips and visits, we could not find any church or group that was an established prophetic community.

One of my friends, Kimberley, decided that we should just create one for ourselves. Four of us were interested and began to meet. We would gather every Sunday night to worship and listen to CDs and DVDs on the prophetic. Some of the people we learned from were Graham Cooke, Bill Johnson, Kris Vallotton, John Paul Jackson, and Patricia King. We also practiced listening to God for ourselves and using our gift of prophecy with each other. We applied principles and verses on the gift of prophecy found in 1 Corinthians 14 and used them as our framework:

"Let love be your highest goal! ...one who prophesies strengthens others, encourages them, and comforts them." (1 Corinthians 14:1a, 3)

67

Simple, straightforward guidelines. We had so much fun! We learned, laughed, cried, and spurred one other on *"to acts of love and good deeds"* (Hebrews 10:24).

A Safe Community

As we journeyed deeply together, every effort was made to make our times of fellowship a safe place to learn, grow, risk, and to make mistakes. Love was our highest goal as a community. We had many opportunities to be vulnerable with each other. I learned that vulnerability was a choice on my part. At any time, I could choose to share deeply with my friends. When I recognized how purely my friends loved me, this choice to risk and share openly and honestly with them became easier.

I quickly learned that hiding was difficult in a community that learns to hear the voice of God. As we began to practice the gift of prophecy, God would show us information about each other. It would sometimes leave us feeling very exposed. Yet, we all recognized the importance of operating within the biblical standard for how the gift of prophecy should be used: in love, strengthening, encouraging, and comforting (1 Corinthians 13:2 and 14:3). No one was allowed to point out sin or correct another with the gift of prophecy. Quickly, our group got very real with each other. I experienced being fully seen, known, and loved by God and by my prophetic friends. This was a beautiful atmosphere for all of us to learn about God, each other, and ourselves.

Learning to abide in Jesus Christ also became an essential pathway for using my prophetic gift. When I had an opportunity to listen to God for someone else, I took the posture of abiding and engaged my spirit with the Spirit of God. It was this posture that activated my resident prophetic gift that gave me the ability to hear God's voice for others.

Over the next six months that we met, each one of us was spiritually and supernaturally transformed. In all my years of spiritual disciplines, nothing in my life accelerated my spiritual journey like being in a prophetic community for an extended period of time. Now, you need to understand the full extent of this statement. I was raised Baptist, learned about spiritual disciplines, practiced them, and made them a part of my daily life. I grew into a mature, strong woman of faith and had made godly choices in my Christian walk. Yet, no single spiritual discipline impacted my spiritual growth as much as being in a prophetic community.

I am a Forerunner

Very early on in our precious times together, Holy Spirit began to speak to Kimberley and myself about being forerunners.

Journal Entry: January 2008

"You are both forerunners, and you are being called out to begin a new thing. Just begin to step forward and just start simply. 'It' doesn't need to be anything big or showy. You are anointed and called to do 'this'."

We sure wished we knew what 'it' and 'this' was. We knew the 'new thing' was related to what we had gone through and were experiencing within our gatherings together. We also knew that the transformation that we had undergone was not just for the four of us. If prophetic community had been transformational for us, it would be equally transformational for others. Prophetic community was meant for the Body of Christ. Specifically, for us, the call on our hearts was towards ministering to other women. How could we draw other women into what we had experienced?

This identity of being a forerunner was resonating in my spirit. A forerunner is a person who goes into new places and creates something new for others to follow and then become a part of. Being a forerunner was why I was discontented in maintaining existing groups and Bible studies. I was designed to dream with God and to explore the possibilities of life in Jesus in line with biblical principles. I was created to step into new territory – to risk, try new things, experiment, and create something new with God.

Spirit School

In a desire to step into the 'new thing' that God was calling us to, the four of us decided that, over the summer, we would teach our children what we had learned in our prophetic times together. We had eleven children between the four of us ranging from age three to thirteen. We had a vision for an amped up Vacation Bible School with a focus on Holy Spirit that we called "Spirit School". We met every morning for a week and taught our children different ways to worship: flagging, dancing, art, worshipping with toy swords, soaking, and singing. Then we taught them how to hear God's voice for themselves and then for each other through the gift of prophecy.

The great thing about teaching children how to hear God's voice is that they are full of faith.[4] Our little group

---

[4] (Matthew 18:3)

easily and eagerly stepped into the spiritual principles that we taught them. By the end of the week, they were begging us to extend Spirit School into the next week! They had tasted and seen the goodness of God[5], and they wanted more. Kimberley and I looked at each other and said, "This was easy! We can do this with women!" And so, Hearts on Fire Ministries was birthed.

Hearts on Fire Ministries

In the fall of 2008, Kimberley opened up her home, and we began to invite women to join us for weekly gatherings. We started small with a group of 6-10 women. We used the model of Spirit School: extended worship with a variety of ways to connect with God in worship, simple teaching on how to hear God's voice, listening to God exercises, and opportunities to practice operating in the gift of prophecy.

As our prophetic community was forged, we began to witness the same supernatural results that we first glimpsed on our Washington conference trip. Women's spiritual journeys were accelerated, spiritual and emotional healing was the norm, identities were forged, and destinies were awakened! Within this community, our women learned to love God, themselves, and each other in a much deeper way.

Through word of mouth, we grew. Hungry women from all denominations and churches joined us. In time, God encouraged us to open our meetings for men to join as well. By 2012, we outgrew Kimberley's living room, and she built a building on her land for us to meet in.

Over time, through ministering at Hearts on Fire, I noticed that the majority of prophetic words that I received

---

[5] (Psalm 34:8)

from Holy Spirit for others were identity and destiny words. I could spiritually see who others were created to be, and I could at times see what they were created to do. This anointing partnered well with my calling of bringing people into the highest level of living and doing.

Yet, after journeying with the prophetic word from Shawn for years, I tucked it away on my bookshelf. I could not see that it was developing to any real degree. Admittedly, my waiting was not always done patiently. Sometimes, Holy Spirit would remind me about the word, and I would then pull it out and read and pray over it once again. However, there were many times that reading the prophecy would frustrate me. I wasn't sure what more I was supposed to do to facilitate this word coming to pass.

Over the five years that I ministered at Hearts on Fire, God did a major work in my heart. Since God had revealed to me just prior to the conference that I was prone to making my ministry an idol, the possibility of having a worldwide ministry created the potential for a large idol in my life to arise and become established. I could feel the pull of this temptation of idolatry, and I knew that if my ministry became an idol, my relationship with God and my family would suffer.

My heart's desire was to be true to God alone with no idols in my life. God saw this yearning of my heart, and it was His desire for me as well. He began to mold my character to bring a godly order to the priorities in my life: God first, family second, ministry last. Pursuing God became my priority, not pursuing my destiny or pursuing the fulfillment of the prophetic word. As a result, I learned how to hold the prophetic word loosely. God was the one who could fulfill it in my life. I just had to keep Him my primary focus.

In 2013, God clearly spoke to me that Hearts on Fire was my transition into my ministry, not my end. He was calling me to leave. He told me that I was called to established Christian institutions. I did not know it at the time, but I was moving into living out my prophetic word.

Deeper

After leaving Hearts on Fire, God opened doors for me within the year in my home of Centre Street Church to run a class that would teach leaders how to hear God's voice for themselves and for each other using the gift of prophecy. Again, the intention was to create a loving and safe, prophetic community. This class was called "Deeper".

This was a new season in my conservative, evangelical church. Through the class, I experienced an openness and hunger for Holy Spirit and His gifts like never before. I was so excited to be a part of what Holy Spirit desired to do within the hearts of people and my church community.

I began to write a manual for the participants to follow. I felt God's smile as Holy Spirit reminded me of Shawn's word: I was *writing* my first manual! Deeper community groups led by others and myself produced the same fruit as the Washington conference trip and in Hearts on Fire. Supernatural growth and transformation occurred in the lives of the participants, and they experienced a deeper love for God, themselves, and for each other.

Harvey had become a huge supporter of my ministry over the years as he saw the good fruit and healing in my life and heard about the lives of others that were changed at Hearts on Fire and Deeper. Whenever I would whine about the lack of money I was making, he would be the one to remind me, "Deanna, we are doing this for an eternal reward, not an earthly reward." He became my biggest cheerleader.

We could always see God's fingerprints as we moved forward. Each year that I was in ministry, Harvey and I would evaluate where we were at financially and then take that information to Father God. Our intention was to rely on our relationship with the Lord to make decisions regarding my career. We did not use my destiny, prophetic word to make decisions for our future.

After completing my manuals in 2015, my pastor encouraged me to have them published. As I pursued this option, my thoughts were, *"I do not know how to proceed towards this. Do I really want to invest money here?"* I knew I would probably do nothing on my own. But God knew what I was thinking, and He knew that I needed some supernatural encouragement.

In the spring of 2016, I was driving on the highway when a large raven flew in front of my vehicle. The raven was carrying something large and white in its beak; it looked like a loaf of bread. As soon as I saw it, I heard the Lord speak to my spirit, *"Just like I supernaturally fed Elijah through the ravens [6], I will supernaturally feed you."* I thought, *"Hmmm...interesting, Lord! Thank you!"*

That night was our last night of Deeper for the season. I was given some thank you cards that contained financial gifts: hundreds of dollars. I was shocked, as I had never received financial gifts like this before. Immediately, God spoke into my spirit, *"I will supernaturally feed you."* I knew that the Lord was encouraging me to pursue investing money into my manuals.

Two weeks later, I contacted Kathleen Mailer from ChristianAuthorsGetPaid.com. She offers a service to

---

[6] (1 Kings 17:2-6)

authors, walking them through the process of publishing a book. In my first telephone conversation with her, I explained what I had created with my Deeper manuals. Upon hearing this, she began to prophesy to me:

"You need to write a book that will accompany your manuals. Your book and manuals will go to all churches, not just the conservative evangelical. This is worldwide. You have heard this before, haven't you?"

I had tears in my eyes as God was revisiting my destiny word from Shawn Bolz through this meeting with Kathleen. He was speaking it over me again through someone I had just met. I was in awe. Now, the choice was mine. Would I continue in my faith journey and write that book?

Harvey and I decided that I had indeed invested valuable time and effort into my Deeper manuals, and thus we should pursue moving its ministry forward and see how God would use them. We both could see God's fingerprints and His encouragement to continue on. After we made the decision to invest in the book and the manuals, more supernatural provision came in and the hundreds of dollars turned into thousands. God's fingerprints turned into His loud cheering, *"I want you to do this!"* His reassurance helped me to push through my multiple fears and insecurities and step into the plans that He had for me.

When I heard for the second time the mention of 'worldwide ministry' from Kathleen Mailer, I was so happy to feel in my heart that this truly did not matter to me. God could do it if He wanted to, but if it didn't materialize, that was just fine with me. I had learned to live in godly order: love God, love my family, and then love others through my ministry. My ministry was whomever God brought into my path and into my Deeper groups. What a joy to live in God's love and His divine order!

My Hope for You

The biblical principles and disciplines that I teach within this book and through my manuals is how Holy Spirit taught me and led me into complete healing and restoration. I am now completely free to live in my identity. Deeper is how I continue to live my life. And I continue to daily journey with Holy Spirit. I am a part of a loving, supportive, prophetic community where I am free to be myself. As I choose to do my part in moving towards my destiny, Father God responds by doing His part — immeasurably more than I could ask or imagine (Ephesians 3:20). I feel so privileged to be chosen as His child and live this adventure called Christianity!

I love the spiritual power of stories telling of God's glory. Testimonies that glorify the power of the Blood of the Lamb release a spiritual principle that overcomes Satan, not only in the storyteller's life, but in the listener's life as well (Revelation 12:11). I pray that, as I have shared my testimony of the power of the Blood of Jesus to save and heal me, you will have a renewed hope as a result and an increased desire for Holy Spirit to lead you in your personal journey.

My hope is that you can see through my story that my God is for me, not against me (Romans 8:31). Moreover, I hope that you will understand and truly believe that this promise is for you as well. Above all, I pray that my journey gives you hope for your life and your future. You are worth fighting for, and a rich, satisfying, more abundant life in Jesus Christ is worth fighting for! I encourage you to engage with the written promises of God and the person of Holy Spirit so that you also can journey into fullness of life in Jesus Christ.

I invite you to actively engage with Holy Spirit to discover the spiritual adventure that He has for your life. Holy Spirit is your guide and your teacher, so He knows how to journey with you very personally. As you read the next part of *Deeper,* I will unpack spiritual disciplines and biblical principles that will be helpful for communing with the Holy Trinity but especially with Holy Spirit. You will also learn spiritual principles in how to hear God's voice for yourself and how to hear God's voice for others through the gift of prophecy.

I pray that you will desire to live in all that you were created to be and that you will move in all that you were created to do! I pray that you taste and see the goodness of the Lord, as well as taste and see your identity and your destiny! I encourage you to embrace change, including the pain it brings at times, and begin to move into fullness of life by engaging with Holy Spirit, Jesus, and Father God.

Trinity

Original painting by Deanna Oelke

"May the grace of the Lord Jesus Christ, the love of God, and the fellowship of the Holy Spirit be with you all." (2 Corinthians 13:14)

This painting simply captures the Trinity interacting as the three in one. Hands represent Father God, Holy Spirit is symbolized as Consuming Fire, and Jesus is shown as the Rose of Sharon.

Chapter 3

The Rhythm of Deeper

The principles, ideas, and guidelines of Deeper have become my rhythm and are how I live my life. The goal of Deeper is to learn principles and spiritual disciplines that will foster an enriched and transformational relationship with Holy Spirit. Whether you are well acquainted with Holy Spirit, or whether engaging with Him is new, there is always a deeper level that you can go.

A relationship with a person takes time as you learn about them. The same is true of your relationship with Holy Spirit. For this reason, I encourage you from this point on to take your time in reading through the chapters and engaging in the listening exercises. Ensure that you make loving Holy Spirit, Jesus, and Father God your priority. Make the spiritual disciplines that help connect you in relationship a part of your life.

When I teach Deeper classes, we meet every two weeks, spacing the complete Deeper teaching over eight months. I find that most people need this amount of time between sessions to practice the spiritual disciplines and principles with Holy Spirit so that the teaching moves from their head and is incorporated into their lives. My suggestion is that you allow yourself one to two weeks to practice the principles within each chapter before moving on to the next chapter. On the other hand, you may find it helpful to read through the complete book and then go back and take your time with the listening exercises and with Holy Spirit. Whatever works best for you! I encourage you to learn and engage with Holy Spirit at the pace that He sets for you.

The Core Principles of Deeper

The following are the biblical principles that are foundational for our Deeper sessions:

1. We believe God speaks.

"My sheep listen to my voice; I know them, and they follow me." (John 10:27)

Deeper operates on the foundational understanding that, as Christians, our spiritual inheritance is to hear the voice of God. Since this belief is our starting place in Deeper, I will not be teaching in depth about this principle. The primary way that God speaks is through the written Word of God – the Bible. God's spoken word always lines up with the truth of the Bible and the character of God.

2. We believe that God can speak to us through others with the gift of prophecy.

"But one who prophesies strengthens others, encourages them, and comforts them." (1 Corinthians 14:3)

1 Corinthians 14:1-25 gives guidelines as to how the gift of prophecy is to be used. Specifically, prophecy is to be used to strengthen, encourage, and comfort others. This is the guideline that is taught and followed as we learn to hear God's voice for others. This means that, in delivering a prophetic word, we should not speak of what is wrong or point out sin in another person.

3. Love is our highest goal.

"Dear friends, let us continue to love one another, for love comes from God. Anyone who loves is a child of God and knows God." (1 John 4:7)

God is Love. All prophetic words should be rooted in the love nature of God and should be spoken from the heart of Father God for His children. As we ask Father God what He loves about His children, He opens our spiritual eyes, and we begin to see each of them through His eyes of love. Furthermore, as we learn about Holy Spirit, hear His voice, and practice operating in His gifts, we want to be strategic in building a biblical, prophetic community of love that will encourage each individual and support the work of Holy Spirit.

4. We believe sincerity of desire releases and increases our spiritual gifts.

"Let love be your highest goal! But you should also desire the special abilities the Spirit gives—especially the ability to prophesy." (I Corinthians 14:1)

This Scripture clearly states that we are to desire the gifts of Holy Spirit but especially the gift of prophecy. Think about the character of God: He is loving, kind, and a good Father who knows how to give good gifts[7]. God would not have us desire the gift of prophecy and then withhold it from us. You may be reading *Deeper* and already have the gift of prophecy. Or, you may not have the gift of prophecy and are reading this book because you desire to receive this gift. Desire on your part is all that is needed to receive the gift of prophecy.

The Rhythm of Worship

"Praise the Lord! Praise God in his sanctuary; praise him in his mighty heavens! Praise him for his mighty works; praise his unequaled greatness! Let everything that breathes sing praises to the Lord! Praise the Lord!" (Psalm 150:1, 2, 6)

"The most important [commandment]," answered Jesus, *"is this: 'Hear, O Israel: The Lord our God, the Lord is one. Love the Lord your God with all your heart and with all your soul and with all your mind and with all your strength.'"* (Mark 12:29-30, NIV)

---

[7] (Matthew 7:9-11)

Worship is an important part of the Deeper experience as it provides space for you to experience Holy Spirit's presence for an extended period of time. Worship is important to hearing God, primarily because worship is relational. The worship experience itself can be a time where Holy Spirit does His deepest work.

Try to have regular worship times on your own with God. During worship, make your goal be one of lavishing your love on Jesus, Holy Spirit, and Father God and to connect deeply with them. Do not allow your feelings to dictate whether you should worship or not. David in the Psalms writes:

"Praise the Lord, my soul; all my inmost being, praise his holy name." (Psalm 103:1, NIV)

Whether it's easy or hard, we need to choose with all parts of our being to worship God. Jesus is always worthy to receive our praise. When we don't feel like worshipping or our circumstances are difficult, and it is subsequently hard to praise God, we are offering a *sacrifice* of praise to our Lord when we choose to worship God despite our feelings.

"Through Jesus, therefore, let us continually offer to God a sacrifice of praise—the fruit of lips that openly profess his name." (Hebrews 13:15, NIV)

Often, when I don't feel like worshipping and choose to worship anyway, I find that worshipping was exactly what I needed. Using the *"fruit of [my] lips [to] openly profess His name"* shifts my attitude and feelings off of my circumstances and myself and onto Jesus. This change of

85

focus also adjusts my mindset, renews my mind, and ultimately brings about a transformation of my soul.

Worship is also my favourite form of spiritual warfare. When Satan is trying to discourage me or is harassing me, I choose to turn on my worship music and use my voice to praise my King Jesus! Worship is a posture of submission to God. When you submit to God and resist the devil, he will flee from you[8].

Trying something different than what you are used to in worship may help you to interact with God in a new or deeper way. Try engaging in worship through art, movement, standing, walking, raising your hands, dance, flagging, etc. Be creative and do something that you enjoy during worship.

The following are suggestions for you as you choose your songs and create a playlist:

- If you are not a musician, you can still create a quality, worship experience. Use iTunes to buy songs and arrange them to create a playlist. Make sure you honour artists for their work and pay for the songs you use. Words for the songs can be easily printed out from websites that provide lyrics so that you may follow along. If you are unfamiliar with worship music, some of my favourite worship artists are: Bethel Music, Hillsong, Jesus Culture, Passion, and Chris Tomlin.
- Be certain that your worship songs are worship songs. There are many songs that are sung as worship songs, but they are not actually songs of true worship. Worship is praising, lifting high, declaring, and adoring whom the Holy Trinity is. Songs that sing

[8] (James 4:7)

about a difficult place that I may be in and what I want God to do for me may help to validate my feelings, but they are not worship. Stay away from songs like this when you are choosing your playlist. If you are unsure about a song, ask yourself, *"When I sing this song, are my thoughts turned towards God and who He is, or does it cause me to think about myself?"* Stick with the songs that cause you to focus on Jesus and off your circumstances.

- Rely on Holy Spirit as you choose your songs. Ask Him questions like: What work do You want to do within me today? What songs capture the essence of worship? What order should these songs be played? Holy Spirit already knows the work that He wants to do. He can give you everything you need to provide the experience that He wants during worship.

- Have one to two songs about Jesus or the cross at the beginning of your worship set. This declares into the atmosphere very clearly whom you are worshipping. Jesus is the way to the Father (John 14:6). I believe that this spiritual principle should be applied to entering into worship. Come to the Father and Holy Spirit through Jesus first.

- Choose songs about thanksgiving and praise. Thanksgiving and praise are the gates through which you enter into His presence (Psalm 100:4).

- Try to choose songs where you are singing *to* God not *about* God. This makes the worship experience much more personal.

- Plan to have a minimum of thirty minutes of worship. Worship time allows you to shift out of the busyness of your day, focus on God, and practice abiding.

Along with designated worship times, think about how you can incorporate worship into your daily routine. Paul in his letter to the Philippians encouraged them in their thought life:

"Finally, brothers, whatever is true, whatever is honorable, whatever is just, whatever is pure, whatever is lovely, whatever is commendable, if there is any excellence, if there is anything worthy of praise, think about these things." (Philippians 4:8, ESV)

Having worship music on as I am driving, cooking, cleaning, exercising, working, etc. keeps me in a consistent posture of openness to God with the godly mindset that Paul encourages us to have.

The Rhythm of Intentional Time with Holy Spirit

1. Journaling

As you journey through *Deeper* and learn how to hear God's voice, I encourage you to write in a journal what you sense that you are hearing. When you have written something down, then you are able to revisit and reread those conversations. Also, journal any prophetic words given to you from others plus Holy Spirit adventures and any significant dreams that you have. I discovered over the years that, when I do not write down significant encounters with Holy Spirit or prophetic words given, I tend to forget the details. When Holy Spirit reminds you of these past events, the details are important to remember.

Another thing that I love about journaling is that I can see my spiritual growth. I can recognize how the Lord has been faithful to me when I reread my older journals. The

Israelites often built altars of remembrance to remind themselves of God's faithfulness to give them strength to continue trusting God in their present trials. The same principle can be true for you with your journal entries. They can be a source of strength and encouragement to you and to others to continue pressing on and fight the good fight.

As I have been journaling over the years, I have found the following helpful:

- Buy a journal at the beginning of every year. I find that as Holy Spirit reminds me of spiritual encounters, I remember them in calendar years. When I have a journal for each year, it helps me to find the journal easily to revisit past experiences.
- Title each journal entry by writing the main idea and the date. For example, when I have a dream, I title it "Dream" and then think of a title for that dream. Titling my entries also makes it easy for me to review past experiences.

2. Reading the Bible

Since all spoken words from Holy Spirit as well as prophetic words that you receive from others need to be measured against the truth of the written Word, it is imperative that you know the Bible. Make reading your Bible a daily part of your routine. Here are some things to consider as you plan your Bible reading:

- Choose a translation that is easy for you to understand. If you are a seasoned Christian, try reading from a translation that you are not as familiar with.

- Choose a passage of Scripture that interests you or that Holy Spirit is directing you to.
- If there are specific verses that Holy Spirit has highlighted to you, memorize them and meditate on them. Biblical meditation is thinking deeply about a selected Scripture to allow it to, not only fill your mind, but to enable Holy Spirit to graft it into your very being. This is different than transcendental meditation where the object is to empty the mind of all rational thought and allow the mind to dwell on whatever ideas just happen to enter.
- Listen to an audio recording of the Bible. Many Bible apps have an audio component to them.
- If reading the Bible is not enjoyable for you, ask God to give you a love for His Word.

3. Meditation Process

Whatever way you choose to read your Bible, you may want to try the following meditation and journaling process as you engage with Holy Spirit:

- Invite Holy Spirit into your time with Him. In the stillness, worship the Lord.
- Select, or have Holy Spirit select, a passage from the Bible.
- Read the passage two times.
  - Listen for pieces that grab you and let them sink in.
  - Meditate. What stands out?
  - What word or phrase is highlighted?
- Read the passage two more times.
  - What are you discerning, hearing, or feeling?
  - What is the theme?

o Does the passage rekindle memories or bring to mind certain experiences?

o What is Holy Spirit saying to you?

- Read the passage again.

o Is there something God is calling you to do?

o Tell God what this Scripture is leading you to think about. What are God's thoughts?

4. Space and Time

One of the spiritual disciplines that I learned through my Baptist upbringing was creating space and time in my day to be with the Lord. Traditionally, this could be reading a spiritual book or a devotional book, doing a Bible study, and praying. Allow Holy Spirit to also lead you out of your devotional box or quiet time box. Try different ways of spending time with Him. The intention here is to have times with Jesus, Father God, and Holy Spirit that connect you in relationship. Here are some ideas to explore and activities to invite Holy Spirit, Jesus, and Father God into:

- Spend time in nature
- Take communion
- Read liturgical or repetitive prayers
- Pray in tongues
- Go for a run or a walk
- Rest and be still
- Fast from food or an item of food for a period of time
- Create something

When you find ways that help you easily connect with Holy Spirit, then these can be the ways that you choose to engage in when you sense that Holy Spirit wants you to spend time with Him.

The Rhythm of Biblical Community

North American society values and esteems independence. God does not. God values interdependence. He values us operating as the church in true and rich, biblical community. Ideally, a biblical community should be a place where people have freedom to be themselves, they are loved unconditionally, people are authentic and willing to be vulnerable with each other, and they encourage each other to continue to grow deeper in their relationship with God.

Although the Deeper journey can be done in isolation — one-on-one with you and Holy Spirit — there is enrichment, acceleration, and a depth in your relationship with Holy Spirit that can be encountered within biblical community. Experiencing a rich, biblical, prophetic community during your Deeper walk is invaluable. If you are reading this book and working through the Deeper journey on your own without a trusted group of people, I encourage you to find at least one other person to read *Deeper* and journey with you. Try to find a friend that is hungry for journeying with Holy Spirit and who is interested in hearing God's voice for themselves. At the very least, find someone that you can process with and share what you are learning.

I understand that there are seasons of life where we find that we are alone and cannot seem to find 'iron sharpens iron' friends. If you are in a season like this, allow Jesus to be your friend. Furthermore, pray that He will send you like-minded Christians to journey deeply with you.

Structure of Deeper

Each of the following chapters of *Deeper* will include:

1. Teaching

The teaching of Deeper is biblically based and designed to be easy for you to learn, and then, in turn, easy for you to reteach to your friends. A natural response of people within Deeper is to teach others the principles that have personally impacted them.

2. Listening Exercises

Throughout *Deeper*, you will be given regular opportunities to practice hearing God's voice. Active involvement and engagement in each session is necessary. *Deeper* is not a 'sit back and learn' while you read the book, but rather it's a 'jump in and practice' experience. You will be taking risks and making yourself vulnerable while actively engaging in each session. When you fully involve yourself, you will grow!

The listening exercises are simply suggestions. Ask Holy Spirit for other listening exercises or use your own creative ideas. The point is to practice hearing God's voice for yourself.

3. Going Deeper

Often, I find that people like extra ideas to help them implement the teaching that they had within the Deeper encounter. The "Going Deeper" exercises are suggestions that will help you in further practicing the principles that have been taught, and they may even introduce new principles or spiritual disciplines to help you engage with Holy Spirit at an even deeper level.

Ready? Let's go Deeper with Holy Spirit!

Deeper - Part 1

Hearing God's Voice for Yourself

The Lord is My Righteousness

Original painting by Deanna Oelke

"Blessed are those who hunger and thirst for righteousness, for they shall be satisfied."
(Matthew 5:6)

The dictionary defines righteousness as "morally upright; without guilt or sin". As Christians, this should be how we want to live our lives. But the Bible says that all our righteous acts are like filthy rags! How, then, can I live a righteous life without sin? The key is Jesus Christ and the power of the cross – living in Jesus and Jesus living in me.

Chapter 4

Abiding in Jesus

Another word that is used in Bible translations for abide is "remain". We are to remain in Jesus. Abiding or remaining in Jesus means to be in a connected relationship with Him.

The principle and practice of abiding in Jesus is important as it teaches you to tune your spirit to the Spirit of God. Abiding, then, becomes a pathway in learning to hear God's voice. Many Christians may have already learned how to abide in Jesus, but they do not articulate it as abiding. For example, people who are worshippers naturally engage in a posture of abiding within a worship setting. Abiding is meant to be a lifestyle posture within Jesus, not an event or experience. It is something that you practice on a regular basis so that you can learn how to commune continuously with the Lord.

Before we learn about abiding, I want to distinguish between spirit, soul, and body. We are made up of three parts: body – which is our physical body, soul – our mind, will, and emotions, and our spirit – the truest part of who we are. Although some Scriptures as well as preachers use the term soul and spirit interchangeably, the following two Scriptures[9] make a clear distinction between the soul and the spirit:

"May God himself, the God of peace, sanctify you through and through. May your whole <u>spirit, soul and body</u> be kept blameless at the coming of our Lord Jesus Christ." (1 Thessalonians 5:23, NIV)

For the word of God is alive and powerful. It is sharper than the sharpest two-edged sword, cutting between <u>soul and spirit</u>, between joint and marrow. It exposes our innermost thoughts and desires." (Hebrews 4:12)

For the teaching in *Deeper*, I will use the term spirit and soul in the following ways:

<u>Our Spirit</u>

Our spirit is the truest part of who we are, is eternal, and will continue living on once our bodies have died. Our spirit is what makes us distinctly different from animals. Most importantly, it is how we are uniquely made in the image of God (Genesis 1:27) for God is spirit (John 4:24a).

---

[9] (Emphasis mine)

In the Garden of Eden, when God created Adam and Eve with a spirit, they had a spirit or a spiritual connection with Him, possessing the ability to commune and talk with God directly. When Adam and Eve sinned, they lost that spiritual connection with God. Because of Jesus Christ, it has been made possible to be 'born again' of God's spirit (Ephesians 2:4-5, 1 Corinthians 5:17). Through Jesus' death and resurrection, we can re-establish a spiritual connection with God.

<u>Our Soul</u>

"He restores my soul; He leads me in the paths of righteousness for His name's sake." (Psalm 23:3, NKJV)

Our soul is our mind, our will, and our emotions. It is where pain, rejection, fear, hurts, and memories are. In this Psalm, David states that our soul needs to be restored. It is not born again in the same way the spirit is as we read about in John 3. Instead, our souls can be restored through ways such as obeying the truth through God's Spirit (1 Peter 1:22-23) and by the renewing of our mind (Romans 12:2). Restoring our soul is an ongoing process, whereas having our spirit born again is what happens instantly when we become saved and accept Jesus Christ as our Saviour and Lord.

Worshiping God and Engaging our Spirit

"But the time is coming—indeed it's here now—when true worshipers will worship the Father in spirit and in truth. The Father is looking for those who will worship him that way. For God is Spirit, so those who

worship him must worship in spirit and in truth."
(John 4:23-24)

God, Jesus, and Holy Spirit are spirit beings, and we commune and worship them with our spirits. Similarly, abiding in Jesus is when our spirit remains connected with the Spirit of Jesus, and the Spirit of Jesus remains connected with our spirit. This is called communion.

Worship is one of those intimate times where we practice abiding in Jesus. The principle and practice of abiding helps us tune into how our spirit communes with the Spirit of Jesus as well as tune into how God speaks to us personally. Holy Spirit is available to tutor us in this. He plays a specific role in teaching, training, and equipping us in Spirit-to-spirit worship.

The Principle of Abiding

Before we learn how to abide, let's read and reflect on the following invitation from Jesus:

"I am the true vine, and My Father is the vinedresser. Every branch in Me that does not bear fruit He takes away; and every branch that bears fruit He prunes, that it may bear more fruit. You are already clean because of the word which I have spoken to you. Abide in Me, and I in you. As the branch cannot bear fruit of itself, unless it abides in the vine, neither can you, unless you abide in Me.

"I am the vine, you are the branches. He who abides in Me, and I in him, bears much fruit; for without Me you can do nothing. If anyone does not abide in Me, he is cast out as a branch and is withered; and they

*gather them and throw them into the fire, and they
are burned. If you abide in Me, and My words abide
in you, you will ask what you desire, and it shall be
done for you. By this My Father is glorified, that you
bear much fruit; so you will be My disciples.*

*"As the Father loved Me, I also have loved you; abide
in My love. If you keep My commandments, you will
abide in My love, just as I have kept My Father's
commandments and abide in His love."* (John 15:1-10,
NKJV)

Can you hear the spiritual truths, commands, and
beautiful promises from this passage on abiding in Jesus?

- Father God desires that I bear fruit, so He is willing
  to prune me so that I may bear more fruit.
- I cannot bear fruit by myself. I must abide in Jesus.
- I will bear much fruit by abiding in Jesus.
- I can do nothing apart from Jesus.
- If I abide in Jesus, and His words abide in me, I can
  ask whatever I wish, and it will be done for me. This
  speaks of an intimate communion and conversation
  with Jesus as part of my relationship with Him.
- Father God is honoured and glorified when I bear
  much fruit, and in bearing fruit, I show myself to be a
  true disciple of Jesus.
- Jesus loves me as the Father has loved Him.
- I must abide in Jesus' love.
- I can abide in Jesus' love by keeping His commands.

Why does Jesus teach this concept of abiding in Him and
in His love? Let us read further and listen to His
explanation:

"These things I have spoken to you, that My joy may remain in you, and that your joy may be full. This is My commandment, that you love one another as I have loved you. Greater love has no one than this, than to lay down one's life for his friends. You are My friends if you do whatever I command you. No longer do I call you servants, for a servant does not know what his master is doing; but I have called you friends, for all things that I heard from My Father I have made known to you. You did not choose Me, but I chose you and appointed you that you should go and bear fruit, and that your fruit should remain, that whatever you ask the Father in My name He may give you. These things I command you, that you love one another." (John 15:11-17, NKJV)

Hear Jesus' intention behind this invitation to abide in Him – that you would have intimate <u>friendship</u> with Him! Abiding in Jesus, remaining in His love, and being His friend requires applying energy to the relationship and obedience on our part.

"If you keep my commands, you will remain in my love..." (John 15:10a, NIV)

"You are my friends if you do what I command." (John 15:14, NIV)

Obedience to God is obeying Him in our words and our actions, and it is a submissive posture or attitude on our part. A submissive posture of surrender and obedience is saying "yes" with all of who we are in response to all of who God is. The same is true of abiding in Jesus. Abiding in

104

Jesus is simply saying "yes" to Jesus with every part of our being: our spirit, soul (mind, will, emotions), and body.

Most Christians have experienced a time in their relationship with Jesus when they have felt very close to Him, thus experiencing the result of abiding. You may have sensed Jesus' presence in a very tangible way, felt His love invade your emotions, or felt a deep, Spirit-to-spirit connection with your friend Jesus. Or, you may have experienced a deep knowing in your mind and more of an intellectual communing with Jesus. Sometimes, it helps to reflect on past seasons in your life when you have connected deeply with Jesus to help you readily step into His presence and into abiding.

The Practice of Abiding

As the following steps to abiding are important, consider memorizing them. Being familiar with the process will help you, especially as you will be encouraged to practice abiding throughout the rest of the book, particularly with the listening exercises.

We are now going to practice abiding in Jesus. Take your time, relax, and enjoy your time with Him. Consciously choose to engage the following parts of your being with Jesus:

- Your body: Choose a body posture (body language and position) that communicates a "yes" to Jesus.
- Your soul:
  o Your will – Choose to say "yes" to Jesus. Choose to trust Him. It all starts with a choice.
  o Your mind – Say "yes" in your mind and then follow up by speaking it out loud to Jesus in a verbal declaration.

105

o Your emotions – Say "yes" to Jesus with your feelings or your heart. Allow yourself to emotionally connect.
- Your spirit: Your spirit is the truest part of who you are. From the depths of your being – your spirit – communicate a "yes" to Jesus and all that He is.

From this posture of abiding – a place of submission and openness to Jesus – you are now ready to commune with Jesus using the following prompts:

- Express your love to Jesus:
  o Through your mind
  o Through your emotions
  o Through your spirit
- Receive love from Jesus:
  o Into your spirit
  o Into your emotions
  o Into your mind
  o Into your will
  o Into your body

Reflection

There you go. That is the posture and practice of abiding. The posture of abiding is simply saying "yes" with your spirit, soul (mind, will, emotions), and body. The practice of abiding is staying in that posture, that place where you have an attitude of submission, openness, and expectancy.

What was this practice like for you? Did you sense the presence of Jesus and His love in this posture? Maybe you had a strong sense of spiritual connection as you took this stance, or maybe your sense was subtler. Even if you had no tangible feeling of connection with Jesus, then choose by faith − as you submit your whole spirit, soul, and body to Jesus − to believe that you were indeed abiding with Him. Continue to be expectant. Jesus delights in communing and connecting with His children in this manner.

These steps are a practical way that you can prepare your spirit to abide in the Spirit of Jesus before you enter into any intentional time with the Lord like in worship or through your devotions. When you know how to abide, you can step into it more quickly and easily. With practice, you can learn to live in a daily posture of abiding.

Living in a Posture of Abiding

One of the promises of abiding and remaining in Jesus is that you will bear much fruit: love, joy, peace, patience, kindness, goodness, and gentleness. There will be times when you feel the presence of Jesus and see fruit rather quickly. At other times, however, you won't see the fruit develop quickly at all. Keep in mind that some fruit grows and makes itself evident over time.

Don't rely on your emotions or physical sensations as an indication of abiding. If you are coming to Jesus in a posture of submission and obedience, choose to believe by faith that your spirit is abiding in the Spirit of Jesus. Many times, Jesus wants to teach us to come to Him by faith and not rely on our emotions or other parts of our being. The key is in resting, trusting, expecting, anticipating, and waiting on Him.

Satan does not want us to abide in Jesus, be led by His Spirit, or bear any fruit. In fact, he will do whatever he can to draw us out of this posture of intimate communion with Jesus. Frequently, he does this by hooking into our soul and distracting us through our feelings or mind. Satan desires us to be led by our mind through things like doubt, scepticism, and lies. Satan may also try to lead us out of a spirit connection with Jesus by having us respond to a situation with uncontrolled feelings such as anger and frustration instead of with self-control. This is where obedience and discipline is necessary to remain in a place of abiding.

Jesus, Holy Spirit, and Father God will lead you through your spirit. With your will, choose to obey Jesus and the Bible and choose to stay in submission to Him and His Word. With your mind, take every thought captive to the obedience of Christ. Although you can value your emotions, you must also use self-control and submission to the Word of God to ensure that Jesus is leading you and you are not being swayed and directed by your emotions. This is how you live in the posture of abiding.

Let me give some practical examples to help illustrate this principle.

Tara's Story

Tara attended my Deeper classes and found the training on abiding to be very impactful for her spiritual growth. The teaching made sense to her as she could recall situations in her past where the Spirit of God led her through a posture of abiding, and then there were those situations where she was not operating from a place of communion with Jesus at all. For Tara, the easiest way that Satan used to get her out of a place of abiding was to hook into her emotions and have her emotions lead her. She found that the awareness and understanding of how to remain in Jesus helped her practice staying in a posture of submission and obedience to Him.

After developing the practice of abiding in her life, things changed. When she began to feel frustrated, hurt, or angry in a situation, she chose not to lash out but would exercise self-control instead. She began to engage with Holy Spirit and the written Word of God that she had hidden in her heart to respond in a godly way.

Through the changes God was working out in her life, Tara found that her conversations with others were impacted by her choice to abide. When she would have a conversation that did not turn out well, she would honestly reflect and subsequently realize that she had been led by her emotions once again and not by the Spirit of God. As a result, she began to make a conscience choice as she entered into conversations to allow her spirit to be led by Holy Spirit. She discovered that as she did this, verses would randomly come to her mind, and she would be enabled to speak with wisdom.

As Tara grew in the practice of abiding, she experienced boldness and a confidence in the Lord when conversing with others. Holy Spirit would show her how to speak to each person with gentleness and in a personal way that they could hear and receive. People began to respond positively to her and would, at times, seek her out afterwards to tell her what an impact that conversation had on them. Tara knew that this was God working through her as she stayed in an open position of obedience and expectancy with Jesus. She was experiencing beautiful, supernatural fruit in her choice to abide.

Annie's Story

Annie came into my Deeper class when she was in an emotional and vulnerable place in her journey. Some very real and difficult situations in her life had left her broken and wounded. I could see on the first evening we were together that she needed a deep, healing touch from Jesus.

Annie caught a hold of the principle of abiding and communing with the Spirit of God. In her emotionally vulnerable state, she chose to trust God and daily practice abiding. Our Deeper class was delighted to hear Annie give testimony at every Deeper session as to what she was learning and how she was experiencing Father's love. We could see every two weeks that Annie was being supernaturally transformed. The fruit in her life was abundant and evident to all of us! Her healing journey was accelerated by her choice to trust and take a posture of abiding in Jesus.

Annie describes how she learned the posture and practice of abiding. God showed her that, in the past, she had gone to others to have her needs of love met. God revealed to her that human love was like a shallow bucket of love that empties quickly. Yet, His love was like a waterfall, vast and never-ending! This is her journal entry related to this concept:

"Truth discovered is far more powerful than truth told. This is what I discovered in my journey over the past months as I spent more and more time in the presence of God and let the truth of His Word soak in.

"He is the author and creator of love. His love is like a waterfall, never-ending. He fully understands love, and He freely lavishes me with His love if I allow Him access to my heart. Human love is like a small bucket, which is limited. When I realized I could go to the never-ending waterfall to fill my love tank, the bucket became insignificant. My truth is: God fills my love tank. I am then free to love the people that God

places in my path each day without an expectation of needing or wanting something in return. I can let go of people-pleasing because I am secure in the everlasting love of my Heavenly Father.

"I have always been a doer; that had been my default to survive. Something beautiful occurred when I stepped into abiding. I felt this incredible sense of relief. A relief that I could just 'be'. I'd never been given permission to just 'be' or given myself permission to just 'be'. My spirit had always been hungry for this posture, but life had demanded (or I had believed that life demanded) that if I let go of doing, everything would fall apart.

"In reality, everything had to fall apart for me to begin to heal and to step into freedom. What I didn't realize until later is that it was in the 'being' that Abba Father was able to gently begin the process of removing the walls of self-protection I had built up. In abiding, a safety and trust began to occur in my spirit. I began to trust that Abba Father was a good Father, and He began to show me truth and replace the lies I had believed about my identity and about who He was as my Heavenly Father. Healing came through just 'being'. It was His presence that healed. My part was to come – come with my brokenness and 'be'."

Listening and engaging in worship music was very healing for Annie. She would often spend hours soaking in His presence as she listened to the songs. As she allowed herself to just 'be' in His presence, she would imagine herself under the waterfall of God's love and would posture herself to receive her Heavenly Father's love. In the past, she had been a doer, but as she learned to just 'be' and allowed the words of the Lord to wash over her spirit, she realized the freedom and the healing that took place without any effort of her own. It was during these times that she felt closest to God. In the beginning, she intentionally imagined herself standing under the waterfall with her arms open wide and her head tilted back in an attitude of total surrender and abandon as the water of His love gently flowed over her brokenness. When she found a worship song that deeply impacted her and spoke to her spirit, she would play it over and over, soaking in the words of the song as she basked in the love of Abba Father. One song that particularly ministered to her during this time was "Come to Me" by Bethel Music.

These are two practical examples of how positioning your spirit to abide in the Spirit of Jesus can be used in daily life. Learning to abide in Jesus can become a constant and consistent posture from which we live our Christianity.

Listening Exercise

Soaking in Father's Love

"He [the Lord your God] will rejoice over you with singing!" (Zephaniah 3:17b, NKJV)

I love the imagery of this verse. Whenever I think of this verse, I remember the times that I have watched a mother or father hold their baby. The love they have for their child is evident by the expression on their face and the little and endearing words that they speak over the child. Their love for their baby is in full expression when they spontaneously break out in song, communicating their love for their child. This child has done nothing to earn either parent's love. The love is just there, strong and beautiful.

This image of human love provides a small picture into Father God's love toward us. We do not have to do anything to earn His love, for there is nothing we can do that would cause Him to love us less, and there is nothing that we can do for Him that would make Him love us any more than He already does. God's love is so deep for you that He breaks out in song and rejoices over you[10]. Delighting in *who you are,* God rejoices in your *being* without you having to do a single thing!

For this listening exercise, you will posture yourself to abide in Jesus. Then within the love of Jesus, you will posture yourself for Father God to rejoice over you with singing. This listening exercise will take some preparation on your part.

---

10 (Zephaniah 3:17)

1. Create a playlist of songs that have been written as if Father is singing them to you. Here is a sample playlist of songs that can be purchased on iTunes:
   - "Come Away" – Jesus Culture
   - "Rest" – Beckah Shae
   - "Come to Me" – Bethel Music
   - "I knew What I was Getting Into" – Misty Edwards

2. Now add a few songs to your playlist that reflect a response on your part to the love of Father God:
   - "Good, Good Father" – Housefires
   - "Great I Am" – New Life Worship
   - "I Belong" – Kathryn Scott
   - "No Longer Slaves" – Bethel Music

3. Create a playlist that is at least thirty minutes in length. You could also choose to create a playlist that is just instrumental music.

4. Find a comfortable place to sit or lay down.

5. Take a posture of abiding and consciously choose to engage your body, soul (mind, will, and emotions), and spirit in the practice of abiding – saying "yes" to Jesus – as outlined previously in this chapter.

6. Play your songs and fully engage in the love of Father God.

Take time now to reflect. As you were abiding, did you sense any fruit of Holy Spirit? Did you perceive His presence? Was He speaking to you? Journal with Holy Spirit, Father God, and Jesus about your times of abiding with Him.

Going Deeper

Extra Practice

What would it be like if you chose to say "yes" to Holy Spirit, Father God, and Jesus with all of who you are every moment of the day? If this is your desire, the following is a prayer that you can pray regularly:

"Father, I choose to be a spiritual woman/man of God. I desire to walk all the days of my life in Holy Spirit. In Jesus' name, I command my body, mind, will, and emotions to submit to my spirit, and I command my spirit to submit to Holy Spirit of the mighty Jehovah God. I choose to receive no strength, help, support, or guidance from any other spirit other than Holy Spirit of God in Jesus' name. Amen."

It is important to practice engaging your whole being (body, soul, and spirit) with Jesus before you have your personal times with God. Also, practice connecting with Holy Spirit, Father God, and Jesus throughout the day and when you communicate and interact with other people. The more you say "yes" to Jesus with all parts of who you are and through daily practice, the easier it will become.

At the end of your devotional time, or at the end of your day, reflect on what this was like and journal any significant words that God spoke to you or any experiences that you may have had as a result.

Freedom

Original painting by Deanna Oelke

"The Spirit of the Sovereign Lord is on me, because the Lord has anointed me to proclaim good news to the poor. He has sent me to bind up the broken hearted, to proclaim freedom for the captives and release from darkness for the prisoners."(Isaiah 61:1, NIV)

Before painting this picture, God had been speaking to me often about butterflies. As I questioned Him, I realized that He wanted to speak to me about freedom. Jesus has the power to transform a life. As this transformation takes place, there is such newfound freedom to be beautifully authentic! In this painting, the woman is aware of the transformation and beauty that is taking place within her, but her attention remains fixed on her first love: Jesus Christ.

Chapter 5

Engaging with Holy Spirit

We all have our own ideas about and experiences with Father God, Jesus, and Holy Spirit. Often, we come with a 'God box', one that contains all our ideas about the Trinity. You may be like I was and have a lack of understanding of and experience with Holy Spirit. Since prophecy is a gift from Holy Spirit, He is an important member of the Trinity for us to learn to engage in relationship with.

One of the things that I have loved throughout my spiritual journey has been getting to personally know each member of the Trinity. In this regard, Holy Spirit has drawn me into the fun nature of the Trinity. Over the years, Holy Spirit has led me into such delightful adventures.

One of my favourite Holy Spirit adventures happened one evening when I was at Hearts on Fire with my daughter, Janessa. This was at the beginning of our ministry when our gatherings were quite small, and we had an out-of-town friend worshipping with us. In the middle of worship, this friend disappeared for a while and then returned weeping, asking if we could pause worship. She began to tell us about her Holy Spirit adventure.

Fifteen years prior, my friend was at a conference where she saw some Jewish scarves for sale. Holy Spirit told her to buy six of them. This was a financial sacrifice for her at the time, but she obeyed. She knew the scarves were not for her but to give away at some point.

In each church that she attended, she would lay them out to be used during worship. Yet, she never felt the Holy Spirit prompt her to give them away to anyone. Eventually the scarves were stored away. When she was packing to come visit us, the bag of scarves fell out of her closet. As soon as they hit the floor, she heard Holy Spirit say, *"Bring the scarves along with you."*

On the airplane ride, she felt the excitement of a 15-year-long, Holy Spirit adventure coming to an end. Holy Spirit told her, *"When you are in a room worshipping with six other women, hand out the scarves to each of them."* We were the group of six women, Janessa included.

What a beautiful experience to be a part of her Holy Spirit adventure! As she gave each of us a coloured scarf, Holy Spirit gave her an encouraging, prophetic word for each of us. My mother's heart was thrilled that Janessa could be a part of this story.

In the morning, I wanted Janessa, along with myself, to share the story with my son, Caleb, who was age 8 at the time. It was my desire that he also could be encouraged by my friend's faith.

As Janessa and I began to tell Caleb about our experience, he interjected, "I know, Mom."

"What do you mean 'you know'?"

"I dreamt about it. You got a white scarf, Janessa got a green one, there was a blue scarf, and someone got a red one. I don't know her name," he replied.

Janessa squealed with delight and began to ask Caleb more questions as she realized that Holy Spirit had supernaturally allowed Caleb, through his dream, to experience our evening with us. And my response? I had to pick my gaping jaw up off the table!

I realized in that moment that I had placed God in a box. My box was bigger and maybe more colourful than other Christians' boxes, but it was still a box. I thought I had God figured out, but God kindly confronted my arrogance. I sensed God encouraging me with this verse: *"For my thoughts are not your thoughts, neither are your ways my ways,' declares the Lord."* (Isaiah 55:8, NIV). I repented in humility for restricting God and confining Him to my God box.

Holy Spirit is our guide (John 14:15-17). I believe that one of the best ways that Holy Spirit helps us and guides us is to lead us into deeper relationship with the Holy Trinity. If we are willing, Holy Spirit will draw us into deeper relationship with God. In doing so, He will dismantle the box that we may have constructed to contain God, either in our ideas or through our experiences.

Introduction of Holy Spirit to the Believers

The Jews had a God box containing specific ideas about how the promised Messiah would look and operate on the earth. Jesus ended up looking very different than what they expected, and He behaved contrary to what they imagined. Before Jesus' ascension, He reminded believers that the promised Holy Spirit would be coming. Those believers, too, likely had their own ideas about Holy Spirit and what He would be like.

Let's read about the believers' introduction to Holy Spirit in the book of Acts:

The Holy Spirit Comes

"On the day of Pentecost all the believers were meeting together in one place. Suddenly, there was a sound from heaven like the roaring of a mighty windstorm, and it filled the house where they were sitting. Then, what looked like flames or tongues of fire appeared and settled on each of them. And everyone present was filled with the Holy Spirit and began speaking in other languages, as the Holy Spirit gave them this ability." (Acts 2:1-4)

Meditate on this Scripture passage and reflect. Journal if you like.

- Take a posture of abiding in Jesus, saying "yes" to Him with your body, soul, and spirit.
- Read through the Scripture slowly.
- Listen for pieces that catch your attention. What stands out to you? Let them sink in.
- What word or phrase is highlighted?

- What is this Scripture leading you to think about? Tell God your thoughts.
- How did Holy Spirit make Himself known to the believers on the day of Pentecost?
- This was a powerful, experiential, supernatural encounter that they had with Holy Spirit. What are some of your feelings when you think about having a powerful, experiential, supernatural encounter with Holy Spirit? Why?
- What do you know about Holy Spirit? Who is He personally to you? How is He different or the same as Father God and Jesus?

The Activity of Holy Spirit

Meditate on the following verses regarding the ministry of Holy Spirit:

He Teaches

"But when the Father sends the Advocate as my representative—that is, the Holy Spirit—he will teach you everything and will remind you of everything I have told you." (John 14:26)

"For the Holy Spirit will teach you at that time what needs to be said." (Luke 12:12)

He Gives Life

"The Spirit alone gives eternal life. Human effort accomplishes nothing. And the very words I have spoken to you are spirit and life." (John 6:63)

He Intercedes

"And the Holy Spirit helps us in our weakness. For example, we don't know what God wants us to pray for. But the Holy Spirit prays for us with groanings that cannot be expressed in words." (Romans 8:26)

We are Filled by Him

"And everyone present was filled with the Holy Spirit and began speaking in other languages, as the Holy Spirit gave them this ability." (Acts 2:4)

Holy Spirit may be calling you to a deeper place of surrender and trust in who He is, His ways, and the work that He desires to do within you. Whatever your relationship with Holy Spirit is like, there is always a greater depth you can go. If you desire a deeper relationship with Holy Spirit, express this desire to Him. If you have concerns, confess these to Him as well. If you recognize that you have a God box, surrender your box to Him. Express your trust in Him – in who He is and in His ways. It is in this place of pursuing relationship in an attitude of trust and yielding to Him that you can go deeper.

Engaging with and Listening to Holy Spirit

As we engage with Holy Spirit and listen to Him, we can take the posture of abiding where our spirits commune with the Spirit of God. This heart attitude is one of openness and submission to Father God, Jesus, and Holy Spirit. As we take this stance, it allows us to be sensitive to any way that Holy Spirit may choose to interact with us, for we are purposefully positioning ourselves to invite Holy Spirit to invade our space.

The posture of abiding can also be more active on our part. As we intentionally listen to Holy Spirit, we can press into Him, His voice, and ensure that we are receiving all that He wants to give us. We can also invade His space in our pursuit of this deeper relationship.

Reflect on these verses from Romans 8:

"And the Holy Spirit helps us in our weakness. For example, we don't know what God wants us to pray for. But the Holy Spirit prays for us with groanings that cannot be expressed in words. And the Father who knows all hearts knows what the Spirit is saying, for the Spirit pleads for us believers in harmony with God's own will. And we know that God causes everything to work together for the good of those who love God and are called according to his purpose for them." (Romans 8:26-28)

When we ask Holy Spirit what He is praying for us, we simply need to pray in agreement with what He reveals as God's will and then cooperate with the work that He wants to do in our life. We can ask Holy Spirit at any time what He is praying to Father God on our behalf. This can be particularly beneficial upon entering new seasons in our journey (a new year, new job, new ministry, etc.).

Preparing to Actively Listen to Holy Spirit

We hear, sense, and perceive from three different sources: God, Satan, and ourselves. As we prepare to hear the voice of God, it is important to pray that it is God's voice that we are listening to.

1. Through the name of Jesus, we can silence the voice of Satan: "In the name of Jesus, I silence the voice of any spirits that are contrary to Holy Spirit."

2. As we prepare our spirit, soul (mind/imagination, will, emotions), and body to hear God's voice, we pray a prayer of submission: "I joyfully submit my spirit, soul, and body to You, Holy Spirit." We must not turn ourselves 'off', for God can communicate through all parts of our being when He speaks to us.

3. Our imagination/mind is one way that God speaks to us. Sometimes, we are exposed to images, sounds, and experiences that 'dirty' our imagination and interfere with hearing and seeing from God through our minds. Ask Jesus to clean up your imagination. Ask Him to forgive you, if necessary, and to wash away all the unholy things you have seen, heard, or experienced.

4. After asking Holy Spirit questions, by faith, choose to believe that the words, thoughts, pictures, images, and senses that follow are from Him: "I welcome You, Holy Spirit, to speak to me. I declare that I am God's child, and I hear His voice. I trust that what I receive will be from You."

When you are beginning to hear Holy Spirit's voice, it is easiest to start by asking Him questions. When you ask Him a question, write down what you sense, hear, or perceive that He is saying. Keep writing until you sense that He is done 'speaking'. Then, ask Him more questions about what He has said to you. Ensure that you have heard everything from Holy Spirit.

As you are listening, make certain that your mind stays submitted to your spirit. It is very easy for your mind to stop the flow of Holy Spirit speaking. Take the approach that you are receiving a dictation; purely write what you are hearing. After you sense that Holy Spirit is done speaking, then rely on your mind to help discern what you have written, making sure that it lines up with the truth of the Bible and the character of God.

When listening to Holy Spirit, you may know immediately that it is Holy Spirit speaking. In these moments, it is easy to receive the words from Holy Spirit. But sometimes, it is not as obvious. In those instances, the dictation that you wrote down may feel more like yourself. A common question in these types of encounters is: "How do I know whether it is my voice speaking or Holy Spirit's voice?" If it is your voice, yet what you received is in line with the Bible and with the character of God, then at the very least, you are encouraging yourself in the Lord! There is no harm in this. We all have 'encouraged ourselves' at some point. If Holy Spirit was speaking, you will see fruit at a level that is greater than self-encouragement (love, truth, life, and fruit of the Spirit). Keep in mind that sometimes it is only with time that you see the fruit of Holy Spirit develop. If, with time, you see good fruit resulting from that word, realize that it was indeed God's voice speaking into your life. Upon that realization, remember and reflect on what it was like when you received that word from the Lord. This will help you tune in to how He speaks to you and thus refine your sensitivity to His voice. Remember: God's voice is pure and holy, and it will never contradict the Bible or His character.

Listening Exercise

Jesus Walking on Water

Our listening exercise today will take us into the story of Jesus and Peter walking on water. Just as Peter chose to have faith to walk on water and step into new territory, so can you choose to have faith to step into new, spiritual places.

Pray the following prayer to prepare yourself to hear God's voice:

"In the name of Jesus, I silence the voice of any spirits that are contrary to Holy Spirit. I joyfully submit my spirit, soul, imagination, and body to You, Holy Spirit. I welcome You, Holy Spirit, to speak to me, and I declare that I am God's child, and I hear His voice."

Firstly, you are simply going to read through the following Bible story:

Jesus Walks on Water

Immediately after [the feeding of the five thousand], Jesus insisted that his disciples get back into the boat and cross to the other side of the lake, while he sent the people home. After sending them home, he went up into the hills by himself to pray. Night fell while he was there alone.

Meanwhile, the disciples were in trouble far away from land, for a strong wind had risen, and they were fighting heavy waves. About three o'clock in the morning Jesus came toward them, walking on the

128

water. When the disciples saw him walking on the water, they were terrified. In their fear, they cried out, "It's a ghost!"

But Jesus spoke to them at once. "Don't be afraid," he said. "Take courage. I am here!"

Then Peter called to him, "Lord, if it's really you, tell me to come to you, walking on the water."

"Yes, come," Jesus said.

So Peter went over the side of the boat and walked on the water toward Jesus. But when he saw the strong wind and the waves, he was terrified and began to sink. "Save me, Lord!" he shouted.

Jesus immediately reached out and grabbed him. "You have so little faith," Jesus said. "Why did you doubt me?"

When they climbed back into the boat, the wind stopped. Then the disciples worshiped him. "You really are the Son of God!" they exclaimed. (Matthew 14:22-33)

You are now going to read through the story a second time. As you read, take the posture of abiding. Once in this heart attitude, you are going to listen to Holy Spirit, allowing Him to speak through your thoughts, your imagination, or other parts of your being through the story of Jesus and Peter.

As you read through the story again, pause at times to reflect on the different aspects of the story. Listen, meditate on the story, and employ your imagination to put yourself in the story. Let yourself 'experience' the scene, allowing yourself to have an encounter with Jesus and Holy Spirit as a result.

Let's begin:

Immediately after [the feeding of the five thousand], Jesus insisted that his disciples get back into the boat and cross to the other side of the lake, while he sent the people home. After sending them home, he went up into the hills by himself to pray. Night fell while he was there alone.

Meanwhile, the disciples were in trouble far away from land, for a strong wind had risen, and they were fighting heavy waves.

- Imagine yourself in the boat, fighting heavy waves. What is spiritually fighting you to keep you from getting to where Jesus wants you to go?

About three o'clock in the morning Jesus came toward them, walking on the water. When the disciples saw him walking on the water, they were terrified. In their fear, they cried out, "It's a ghost!"

- In the boat, with the strong wind and heavy waves fighting against you, what emotions rise up? Share any emotions with Jesus.

But Jesus spoke to them at once. "Don't be afraid," he said. "Take courage. I am here!"

- Allow Jesus to speak to any fear: "Don't be afraid. Take courage I am here!"
- Choose to receive courage from Jesus. Allow the truth that Jesus is with you to saturate your body, soul, and spirit.
- Focus on the fact that He is with you in the strong wind and the heavy waves.

Then Peter called to him, "Lord, if it's really you, tell me to come to you, walking on the water."

- Like Peter, choose to step forward in your desire to be closer to Jesus.
- Like Peter, ask Jesus to call to you.

"Yes, come," Jesus said.

- Can you sense Jesus' invitation to follow Him in a new way?

So Peter went over the side of the boat and walked on the water toward Jesus.

- Choose to activate your faith and walk toward Jesus in a new way.

But when he saw the strong wind and the waves, he was terrified and began to sink. "Save me, Lord!" he shouted.

- What doubts or fears distract you from a deeper spiritual walk and relationship with Jesus?

Jesus immediately reached out and grabbed him. "You have so little faith," Jesus said. "Why did you doubt me?"

- Ask Jesus to show you if there is a specific doubt that you have about Him. Ask Him to speak a truth about who He is that will combat this doubt.

When they climbed back into the boat, the wind stopped. Then the disciples worshiped him. "You really are the Son of God!" they exclaimed.

- Worship Jesus in the truth that He has revealed about Himself to you. Allow your faith to rise up in this new understanding of who Jesus is.

Now, immerse yourself in the story for the third time. Imagine yourself in the story sitting in the boat – fighting the waves, seeing Jesus walking toward you, being called by Jesus – and choosing faith instead of doubt in your walk toward Him, etc. Interact with Holy Spirit regarding the following questions:

1. As you are in the boat obediently going where Jesus has asked you to go, who or what is fighting you?

2. What emotions or fears do you sense rising up within you?

3. As you choose faith and walk toward Jesus in a new way, what doubts or fears distract you from walking toward Him?

4. Hearing Jesus ask you, "Why did you doubt me?" what do you say in response?

5. Listen to Jesus' response to your doubt. What truth is Jesus giving you about Himself that will combat this doubt? Speak out loud this truth about who Jesus is each time you feel or hear the voice of doubt want to distract you from moving toward Jesus in a new way.

Journal your experience with Jesus and Holy Spirit. Choose to activate your faith and believe that the first things that you see or hear are coming from Holy Spirit. Begin writing as thoughts, impressions, or pictures are revealed to you. Continue to press your spirit into the Spirit of the Lord (posture of abiding) to ensure that you receive all the information that He wants to give you about each question. After you have written answers down for all the questions, go back and read what you have written. Again, verify that what you have written lines up with the Bible and the character of God.

Going Deeper

Extra Practice

What is Holy Spirit praying for you? Invite Holy Spirit into your Bible reading, and then read and meditate on Romans 8:26b-27:

> *"...But the Holy Spirit prays for us with groanings that cannot be expressed in words. And the Father who knows all hearts knows what the Spirit is saying, for the Spirit pleads for us believers in harmony with God's own will."*

Pray the following prayer to prepare yourself to hear God's voice:

> *"In the name of Jesus, I silence the voice of any spirits that are contrary to Holy Spirit. I joyfully submit my spirit, soul, imagination, and body to You, Holy Spirit. I welcome You, Holy Spirit, to speak to me, and I declare that I am God's child, and I hear His voice."*

Ask Holy Spirit the following questions about these verses. Journal what you are sensing Holy Spirit is saying.

1. As I enter into this Deeper adventure, what are You praying for me Holy Spirit?

2. What do You want to teach me about Yourself?

3. What do You want to teach me about myself?

4. What excites You about my Deeper adventure?

5. How can I cooperate with You, Holy Spirit, for God's will to be accomplished in my life during my Deeper experience?

Now that you are finished listening to Holy Spirit, go back and read what you have written to ensure that what you have received lines up with the Bible and the character of God.

Hearts on Fire

Original painting by Deanna Oelke

"Were not our hearts burning within us while he talked with us..."(Luke 24:32, NIV)

After co-founding a prophetic ministry, I was seeking the Lord for inspiration for a painting that would capture the essence of our ministry. I was worshipping one night when I saw, in vision, a flaming heart with the flames forming a woman worshipping. That vision captured our ministry perfectly.

Chapter 6

Ways that God Speaks

Hearing about different ways that God speaks can create an openness and a desire within us for hearing God in new ways. As we explore the variety of ways that God speaks to His people, we need to remember that one way is not more valid than another. The subtle voice of God is just as valid as the audible voice of God; one just requires more faith on our part. God chooses <u>how</u> He speaks to us. Our job is to receive and accept the way He chooses, and if necessary, engage our faith to believe that He is speaking.

It is common to think and believe that how someone else hears from God is grander than how you personally hear from God. Often, this can be because we have grown accustomed to the subtlety of hearing God's voice and may have dismissed it numerous times, thus diminishing or not recognizing its significance and importance. Begin to tune in to any way that God is choosing to speak to you and practice the faith necessary to believe that He is speaking to you.

"And it is impossible to please God without faith. Anyone who wants to come to him must believe that God exists and that he rewards those who sincerely seek him." (Hebrews 11:6)

Faith should be a constant companion on our spiritual journey. Choosing to enact our faith is a vital part to growing in our ability to hear God's voice clearly, whichever way He decides to speak. Our goal in learning to hear God's voice is to establish and develop relationship with Him. As you listen to God in the exercises, choose to have faith that God will reward you as you earnestly seek Him, believe that He desires to speak to you, and come expecting to hear His voice.

The following is a list of some of the ways that God may choose to speak to you. Sometimes, God will begin speaking to you in a new way once you are open to the possibilities. If you think that God may be trying to speak to you through one of the following ways, do not dismiss it. Instead, pay attention and start asking God questions to discover His intention and heart for communicating with you and subsequently to discern what He is saying.

The Bible

God speaks to us primarily through the Bible. What a privilege to be able to pick up the Word of God at any time to receive encouragement, comfort, and wise counsel! All other ways that God speaks must be weighed against the truth of God's written Word.

I love reading a passage of Scripture that Holy Spirit has directed me to. I know that there will be treasures and wisdom that He wants me to find. When He leads me in this manner, I take a posture of abiding and intentionally meditate on the words to glean what He wants to impart. In other moments of study, I will be reading a passage and a verse will seem to jump off the page and impacts my spirit in a way that I had not experienced before. When this happens, I am experiencing the Word of God as being alive and living (Hebrews 4:12). Regardless of the method, God desires to speak to you and commune with you through His Word.

I am so thankful for all the memory verses that I learned in Pioneer Girls Club and Sunday School as a child. These verses are now hidden in my heart. I often find that God speaks to me with a Bible verse that will just randomly pop into my head. This is Holy Spirit bringing a key verse that I have memorized in the past to my remembrance. I then revisit that verse with Holy Spirit, asking Him specific questions so that I might receive all the revelation that He desires to uncover from the verse.

The Audible Voice

Occasionally, one can clearly and audibly hear the voice of God. God's audible voice usually sounds like it is coming from an external source outside of your mind or body. When God speaks in this way, it usually requires little to no faith to believe God is speaking, for it is very impactful, leaving little room for doubt.

I have heard God's audible voice only a few times in my life. The first time was just after I was becoming more

141

aware of the prophetic. God woke me up in the middle of the night and spoke a Scripture reference over me. He did this with the same reference two more times that same night. He was really trying to get my attention! The next morning, I awoke and instinctively knew that God had spoken – I had no doubt. I looked up the reference, but I did not understand it at all. I began to pursue Him for understanding and wisdom. After months of waiting on the Lord, He revealed to me the explanation. Hearing God's audible voice was just the beginning of the adventure He had for me.

The Still Small Voice

The still small voice feels like your thoughts, and it sounds like it is coming from within your mind or body. Pay attention to random thoughts or people that pop into your head. Instead of disregarding them, press into the Lord and ask Him if He is trying to communicate with you.

This is one of the main ways that God speaks to me personally. When I am asking the Lord questions for myself or for others, I trust that the first thing that comes to mind is from Him. Then, I line up what I have heard with the Bible while at the same time asking Him questions so that I may understand it fully. With every thought that God drops into my mind, I continue to press in to what He wants me to do with it.

Visions

There are different types of visions that God uses to communicate. In the open-eye vision, your eyes are open, and you see a vision at the same time you see the natural. This kind of vision requires little or no faith. In a closed-eye vision, your eyes are closed, and you see a picture in your mind. This feels more like your imagination. Finally, there's the open-eye, spiritual vision. This is where the eyes are open, but you see the picture in your spirit. This may feel more like an impression, and you may not see the picture clearly, but you know what it is.

1. Open-Eye Vision

My son, Caleb, experienced an open-eye vision of an angel once. We were picking up our carpoolers from their house when he looked out the window, and there was an angel. He described that he could see the outline of the angel's body and that it was semi-transparent and blue in colour. The angel just stood there and looked at Caleb. When we drove away from the house, the angel followed our van, leaving a blue streak behind him as he ran. When I asked the Lord what this angel was, He said that it was an angel that was assigned to protect the destiny of our family. This has been a vision that the Lord has used to comfort me over the years. I *know* that He has a plan for us as a family.

2. Closed-Eye Vision

I have always been very creative and imaginative. So, it is not a surprise that God has used my imagination as one of the main ways to interact with me. When I have a sense of an image that God wants to show me, I engage with Him to spiritually see this image in my imagination. Creatively speaking, I picture my imagination like a canvas and wait to see what God will 'paint'. When He is done showing me an image, I then turn my focus to what He has shown me and 'paint' my response. As He and I communicate, God will, at times, 'paint' something else. This way of visually dialoguing with God through my imagination is quite active on my part. I do not sit back passively and just wait for Him to show me everything. Instead, I actively respond.

3. Open-Eye, Spiritual Vision

At the beginning of my journey of hearing God's voice, this was how Holy Spirit would speak to me most of the time. Honestly, I would be so frustrated because this way is so subtle. Every time that Holy Spirit spoke to me, I would have to choose to press in with faith to discover what He wanted to show me. As I experienced the good fruit of these revelations being revealed in my heart, and as others affirmed that He was indeed speaking to me in this way, I just had to accept that I needed to use faith as I listened to God to 'see' this type of vision.

I am so thankful now that God used this way first to train me to hear Him. I now do not need to use faith to believe that Holy Spirit speaks to me in this or other subtle ways. I have been trained to hear even the gentlest of whispers. God knew exactly how I needed to be trained.

Through Feelings

When you are engaging with God, pay attention to feelings that you may suddenly have. There are times when God shares His feelings with you that He has about situations or other people. For example, does your heart abruptly fill with love as you think about someone? Do you unexpectedly feel sad? Are you suddenly overcome with an emotion? Press into God and ask Him more questions about what you are feeling. These sudden or random 'shifts' may indicate a feeling through which He wants to communicate something.

If this is a way that God speaks to you, it can feel overwhelming. My daughter, Janessa, hears God predominantly through her feelings. Many times, when God wants to show her something for someone else, He will have her feel the person's feelings.

Janessa was in junior high when she began to articulate some of her experiences to me. One time, she was in a small group of people when someone came and joined the group. Suddenly, she felt sad. As she shared this with me, I suspected that she was feeling something that God specifically wanted her to feel. I quizzed her and found out that she was not at all sad before the person walked up. I instructed her that God may have been showing her His feelings toward someone, or He could have been showing her someone else's feelings. With some teaching, she was prepared for the next time she had a random feeling. She then could ask God, "Is this feeling from You or from someone else? Is there something that You want me to do or say or pray?" Janessa has a high level of empathy, so for her to hear from God through her feelings is a great way for her to reach out to others with compassion and mercy.

When someone hears God in this way, they are often overwhelmed in group settings. The difficulty is that it can be easy for them to own someone else's feelings for themselves. I tell people who hear God through their feelings to "check yourself at the door". I advise them, when they know that they are going to be in the presence of a group of people, that they take inventory of their feelings *before* they enter that setting. Are they at peace? Do they feel content? If yes, then when they enter the room and suddenly feel anxious, fearful, or another random emotion, they know not to necessarily own it for themselves.

145

Instead, they can begin to ask God questions to discover what He wants to reveal about a person or situation.

I have also found it helpful before attending a group event to pray this simple prayer: "Jesus, I ask that You place Your cross between myself and each person here tonight, so that whatever I perceive, sense, or feel is filtered through Your cross."

Through Impressions

This is a very subtle way that God can speak. It is like a mix of a thought and a feeling, but it's not as clear.

When God speaks to me in this way, I often cannot tell if God is speaking or if I am thinking the thought. When this happens, particularly when I am listening for someone else and am not sure if it is God, I will clearly communicate, "I am not sure if this is me or if it is God, but I am sensing this..." When I start a prophetic word with this kind of lead in, the person will tell me right away if this impression is from me or if it is from God. If they confirm that it is indeed God speaking, then I continue to ask God for more. If it is not accurate, however, I know that it is of my own thought, and I then drop the impression and don't pursue it.

Through Your Body

How does your body physically respond in God's presence or to God's truth? If God wants to highlight something that is said, He may choose to give you a physical sensation, like shivers, a burning sensation, or a twitch. In other moments, God may want you to act on something that He is telling you and will consequently give you a physical

146

sensation to encourage you that He is the one prompting you to do so.

When my friend, Kari, started to regularly hear from the Lord, she began to realize that when Holy Spirit wanted her to know that He was speaking to her, He would give her shivers. The shivers would run up and down her whole body. Occasionally, she would feel the shivers if she was personally receiving something from Holy Spirit, and at other times, it would be when someone else said something that was from God. It was like Holy Spirit was saying, *"Pay attention! I am in this."* When we are in conversation with each other, and she says that she is feeling shivers, we both become more attuned to what is being said, for we recognize that this is a way Holy Spirit catches her attention.

In the season where God was first speaking to me with subtle impressions, I attended a party with casual friends who were not my prophetic friends. As one of these friends was talking, I began to have this impression for her: *"Your significance is not tied to what you do."* It was very simple, but I was afraid to speak it out and risk rejection. As I delayed speaking it out, Holy Spirit began to give me fluttering feelings in my stomach. I still delayed, and Holy Spirit increased the fluttering feeling. I continued to delay, and the physical feeling increased even more. Using my body, Holy Spirit made it obvious that He wanted me to speak. When I began to speak out the simple message to my friend, the feeling in my stomach was so intense by that point that I had trouble speaking. I was a little embarrassed that I was huffing and puffing as I spoke, but my friend communicated to me that this was exactly what she needed to hear.

Holy Spirit used this same method to talk to me the next few times that I was in a group of non-prophetic people. I would receive an impression, and then He would give me the flutter in my stomach to show me that He was indeed speaking to me. As I listened quicker to His promptings, the fluttering eventually stopped, and He would just speak to me with impressions. Throughout this growth period in receiving from Him, I had to make the choice as I transitioned to just receiving the impressions that this was still Holy Spirit speaking.

When you first begin to hear Holy Spirit, He may choose to make it obvious to you by giving you a physical sensation or speak in a way that builds your faith and encourages you to act upon His voice. The temptation here is to rely on this clear indication of Holy Spirit's voice and disregard His subtler ways. Yet, God desires that you become tuned in to *any* way that He desires to speak to you.

Symbols in the Natural World

Pay attention when something specific in your environment catches your eye or when you see something repeatedly. These things could include nature, inanimate things, the time on the clock, specific numbers, etc. The list is endless. This could be God trying to communicate using an object. Most often, He uses objects in a symbolic way.

At the start of Hearts on Fire Ministries, I would look at the clock, and it would often be 11:00, 11:11, or 1:11. I would specifically notice 11 on the clock multiple times a week. I began to pursue God as to the meaning of this number. Was this a verse reference? Was there a meaning to the number 11? I questioned Holy Spirit as to the significance of this reoccurring number.

Over the months that followed, I came across Streams Ministries and found a card that they have regarding dream interpretation. In it, they explained that 11 meant 'transition'. I brought this interpretation to Holy Spirit for

148

confirmation, and I sensed that this was what He was communicating – I was in a season of transition. Over the years that I led Hearts on Fire, I continued to have seasons of seeing 11 multiple times a week. After multiple seasons of this this I thought, *"Good heavens! How many transitions do I have to go through to get where You want me to go, Lord?"*

One night, unknowingly towards the end of my time at Hearts on Fire, I was lost in worship when I happened to glance at my watch. There it was...the number 11 once again. At this point, I must admit I was frustrated with the Lord. I questioned Him saying, *"Four and half years of transitions upon transitions? Seriously? This is hard! I am tired of transitions!"*

Father God responded through my thoughts: *"What if Hearts on Fire is not the end where you will live in your destiny but is your transition into your destiny?"* God had my attention! I had always assumed that I would experience the fulfillment of my destiny within Hearts on Fire Ministries. He continued to speak: *"I desire you to become reintegrated into established, Christian institutions."*

I knew without a shadow of a doubt that this word was from the Lord. This was the affirmation that I needed to know that my time at Hearts on Fire was finished. Within seven months, I was hired part-time at a Christian school to teach in their discipleship program, and I was in conversations with my church leaders to pilot the Deeper program. God had opened doors of favour to transition me into the next season of my life.

Clothes that Someone is Wearing

People often dress how they feel. This is especially true for women. Often, without realizing it, they sense in their spirit that 'something' is happening, and they dress accordingly.

I often receive the start of a prophetic word from clothes or jewellery that someone is wearing. When something catches my eye, I ask God, "Are You drawing my attention to this? Why? What do You want me to say?" If He gives me more information, then I speak it to the person.

When God started to speak to me in this way for others, I would occasionally hear Him tell me in the morning what He wanted *me* to wear that day. One day, the Lord told me to wear what I called my 'Overcomer' t-shirt. It had a picture of a strong-looking woman with 'rise up' written on it. As soon as Holy Spirit said this, I had an immediate sense that I was going to meet someone that day that had hurt me in the past.

I began running my errands and chose to take the posture of abiding to prepare myself for this encounter. I decided that, whomever I saw, I would choose to overcome my feelings of hurt and be more than a conqueror (Romans 8:37). Sure enough, coming out of my doctor's appointment, I came face-to-face in the waiting room with a friend from my past who had listened to gossip and slander about me, pushing me out of her life as a result. Powered by Holy Spirit, I quickly chose to overcome evil with good, smiled at her, and greeted her with a cheerful "hi". I was so thankful that God had prepared me for this encounter so that I could, in the moment, be an overcomer instead of being overcome by feelings of rejection as I remembered the situation from the past.

Through Other Believers

Whenever anyone speaks to you with an encouraging message from the Lord, receive the word, and then take the word to God. Holy Spirit is the expert on you and your life. Use the Bible and Holy Spirit to discern the truth of the word and its relevance to your journey and situation. We will be learning later in *Deeper* how to specifically steward prophetic words that someone gives to you.

Colours

Colours are symbolic and have certain meanings. If you are sensing or seeing specific colours, ask Holy Spirit what the colours symbolize. If you have visions and pictures that involve colour, ask Holy Spirit for details as to what He is saying through the meaning of those colours. Again, like the meaning of numbers, Streams Ministries has study cards available that have colours listed with their meanings. Even when you are using these cards, make sure that you are checking with Holy Spirit for His personal interpretation of the colour that He has shown you.

Dreams

Not all dreams are spiritual dreams. However, when you sense that a dream may be from God, journal it and press in to Holy Spirit to see what it means. Share your dream with trusted prophetic friends, and ask if they have any spiritual insight as to its meaning. We will be discussing dreams and dream interpretation more in depth in *Deeper*. In the meantime, pray that God will speak to you through dreams.

Angelic Visitation

The Bible says that angels are created by God to be ministering angels sent to serve and minister to those who will inherit salvation (Hebrews 1:14). Angels are mentioned over 200 times in the Old and the New Testament. God used angels in the past to minister to His people, and He can do the same today. The Bible also makes it clear that we are not to worship angels but are to worship God alone (Revelation 22:8-9).

As you tune in to how God speaks, you may begin to have visions of angels, see angels in your dreams, or feel the presence of an angel. If you encounter an angel, it is very important that you make Jesus your default. What I mean by this is that you ask Jesus questions about the angel instead of dialoguing directly with the angel itself.

The Bible states that Satan disguises himself as an angel of light (2 Corinthians 11:14). Therefore, it is foolish to believe that an angel cannot deceive me. For this reason, whenever I see or have an impression of an angel in the room, I ask Jesus questions about the angel instead of dialoguing with the angel directly. I know Jesus' voice, and I know that as I ask Jesus questions, He will not deceive me.

I have had angelic encounters manifest in a variety of ways over the years. There have been times when God has informed me that I have an angel assigned to me for a season. When I know this, I watch for the work of the angel in my life and cooperate with what God wants to do. Occasionally, I see angels in vision as I am in different places. When I see them, I dialogue with Jesus, asking questions and cooperating with Him and with what He and Holy Spirit instruct me to do. Then, I have had experiences where I felt the presence of an angel, but I did not see it.

Whenever this happens, the hair on the back of my neck stands on end. I cannot discern if the angel is from God or is a demon – I just know that it is a supernatural being. I especially press in to Jesus and Holy Spirit during these encounters, asking Jesus questions about what I perceive and relying on Holy Spirit for guidance and discernment.

One time while I was sleeping, I felt a very strong tapping on my back. My eyes instantly flung open to see Harvey sleeping in front of me. So, what was behind me? I cautiously turned around, afraid of what I might see...but I saw nothing. I knew *something* had woken me up, so I asked Jesus what it was. He said that this was an angel from God that had been sent to clean up my mind, for I had watched a television show that had defiled my imagination. I submitted to Jesus and the work that He wanted to do through this angel and was instantly asleep. I woke up the next morning knowing that I had been cleansed and with the heightened realization that I needed to be more careful in what I exposed myself to through television.

As you are exploring the different ways that God may want to speak to you, relax and have fun! The focus here is on *relationship* with God, so enjoy your time with Him. If hearing God's voice does not seem to be coming easily for you, keep practicing. Don't become discouraged! Remember that the Bible is the primary way that God speaks to His children. Communing with God through His written Word – the Bible – is full of rewards and builds relationship with Him. Scripture is the tried and true way for communication between you and God.

For some people as they are learning how to hear God's voice, they may not be satisfied to interact with God in the way that He is choosing to speak to them. Instead, they may prefer He speak in a way that is more obvious or easy or desirable. Their thoughts may be, *"I think God spoke to me through an impression, but I want God to speak to me through a vision. When that happens, I will know for sure that it is God speaking."* Resist the urge to barter with God and tell Him how He is to speak to you. Remember, He is the one that chooses <u>how</u> to speak; we simply receive. Receive through whatever way He is speaking, engage your faith as necessary, and enjoy communing with Him.

Listening Exercise

Exploring Ways that God Speaks

The following listening exercise will encourage you to communicate with God and receive from Him in a variety of ways. Some ways may feel very awkward whereas others may feel very natural for you. Move around the list and practice ones that you like first if you must but explore as many as you have time for. Most of all, have fun and enjoy your time with Father God, Jesus, and Holy Spirit!

Pray the following prayer to prepare yourself to hear God's voice:

"In the name of Jesus, I silence the voice of any spirits that are contrary to Holy Spirit. I joyfully submit my spirit, soul, imagination, and body to You, Holy Spirit. I welcome You, Holy Spirit, to speak to me. I declare that I am God's child, and I hear His voice."

As you journal, ask Father God, Jesus, or Holy Spirit the following questions and reflections, activate your faith, and trust that the first thing that you see, hear, or sense is from God. And then ask more questions. Be curious!

This list is by no means exhaustive. Use it to start the dialogue between you and God and add to the list as Holy Spirit leads you. Remember that when you are done listening, to line up what you have received with the Bible and the character of God.

1. The Bible
   - Ask Jesus what Bible verse(s) He would like to speak to you through.
   - Why did He choose this verse or passage for you?

2. The Audible or Still Small Voice
   - Ask God to speak into your thoughts through a still small voice or to speak in an audible voice.
   - Ask Him to remind you of a childhood memory. In your mind, remember the details of this memory. Ask God what He would like to say to you about this memory.

3. Visions
   - Engage your imagination and ask God to show you His heart through it. What does it look like?
   - Ask Him to show you something in His heart that you need.
   - Why do you need this part of His heart?

4. Through Feelings
   - Target your focus to where you feel your emotions. Ask Holy Spirit to give you a feeling that He has right now. Can you articulate what the feeling is?
   - Ask Him questions about this feeling of His. Is it for a situation or a person?

- Is there something that He wants to share with you about His feeling?
- Is there something that He wants you to do in response to what He is sharing with you through this feeling?

5. Through Impressions
   - As this is such a subtle way that God can speak, specifically ask God to impress on you what He loves about you.
   - Why does He love this about you?

6. Through Your Body
   - How has God used your body to talk to you before? Ask Him to reveal times when He has done so in the past.
   - Ask Him to use a physical sensation to speak to you in the future.

7. Symbols in the Natural World
   - Ask God to highlight something in the room. What does He want to say to you using this object?

8. Clothes that Someone is Wearing
   - Ask God to highlight something that you enjoy wearing: clothes, jewellery, etc. Why is He highlighting this? Explore the meaning behind the why and ask Holy Spirit to explain what He is bringing it to your attention.

9. Through Other Believers
   - How has God used others to speak to you in the past? If you are not sure, ask Him to reveal those moments.

- Reflect on the words people have spoken into your life. Do they line up with the Word and God's character? If so, what was God saying to you through those impartations?

10. Colours
- Ask Holy Spirit to show you a colour. What does this colour mean?
- What does He want to say to you regarding this colour?

11. Dreams
- Have you experienced a dream that has struck you as being 'different' with details sticking with you long after you have woken up? Ask God if this dream was from Him or not.
- If God impresses upon you that this dream was from Him, ask God for the meaning.

12. Angelic Visitation
- Ask God to prepare you for an angelic visitation. Be open to however it will manifest (e.g. seen with the naked eye, in vision, in dreams, or just sensed), yet being ready to dialogue with Jesus about this visit so that the enemy does not deceive you.

Reflect on this listening exercise:

Do you see a dominant way that you receive information from God? Which ways are easier for you to perceive God's voice, and which ways are more difficult? The encouragement here is to find at least one way that is the easiest to receive from God and to be open to the breadth of how He may want to communicate with you in the future.

Going Deeper

Extra Practice

Continue to interact with Father God, Jesus, and Holy Spirit to discover different ways that they want to communicate with you. There is usually one dominant way that God speaks to each of His children. Once this way is found, you can continue to press in to God with faith, expectation, and a desire for more. Try engaging different ways to listen to Holy Spirit, asking God questions about yourself and about situations in your life. This will increase your awareness and sensitivity to God's voice in your everyday life.

Garment of Praise

Original painting by Deanna Oelke

Jesus gave me "the garment of praise for the spirit of heaviness." (Isaiah 61:3, NKJV)

This painting is the third in a series on Isaiah 61. The background alludes to brokenness and heaviness that has penetrated the body, soul, and spirit. The fabric represents the garment of praise – the antidote for the burdened, failing spirit.

God has made everything beautiful in its time (Ecclesiastes 3:11). When we allow Jesus to touch our spirit of heaviness and work within us, we can't help but be transformed. The results are beyond what we could do in our own human strength. The results are supernatural!

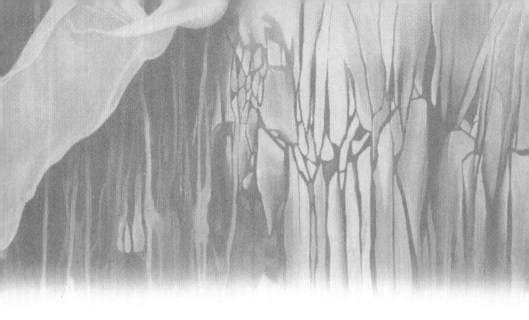

Chapter 7

Continuing to Grow in Hearing God's Voice

"Come close to God, and God will come close to you."
(James 4:8a)

At this point in *Deeper*, I hope you are tuning in to how God speaks to you personally. Once you are confident in hearing God's voice for yourself, it will be much easier to make the transition into hearing God's voice for others when you begin to prophesy. Listening to God and your ability to hear His voice will grow with practice.

At the beginning of your journey of listening to God, there will be moments when God communicates with you and you know without a shadow of a doubt that it is He speaking. God does this on purpose to encourage you and help you tune in to a way that He speaks. In these obvious 'God speaking to you' moments, you do not need to use any of your faith to believe that it is God. You just know it's Him.

Yet, you will find that there will also be times in listening to God where it is more difficult to tell immediately if He is speaking or not. The difference between your voice and God's voice can be very subtle. This subtlety requires you to choose faith and exercise boldness to speak out or act on what you are sensing. Oftentimes, the only way to know if it is God's voice that you are hearing is by acting on what He says or by speaking it out in faith when you are giving a prophetic word to someone else.

"The Lord said, "Go out and stand on the mountain in the presence of the Lord, for the Lord is about to pass by." Then a great and powerful wind tore the mountains apart and shattered the rocks before the Lord, but the Lord was not in the wind. After the wind there was an earthquake, but the Lord was not in the earthquake. After the earthquake came a fire, but the Lord was not in the fire. And after the fire came a gentle whisper." (1 Kings 19:11-12, NIV)

Growing in hearing God's voice is paying attention to subtleties – God's gentle whisper. Many people assume that, as their listening matures, the subtlety of God's voice will disappear. This may not happen. You will likely continue to have times when God's voice is loud, and yet still experience moments when it was still and small. As you continue to press into God, He will continue to come close to you.

As I became more seasoned in hearing God's voice, I found that I still needed to activate my faith and believe that God was speaking to me. Even now, His voice sounds very similar to mine. Choosing faith and engaging desire is a vital part of continuing to grow in hearing God's voice.

Be aware that Satan will try to sow seeds of doubt to keep you from hearing God's voice and deepening your relationship with Jesus. I encourage you to keep practicing listening to God and being open to all the ways He can choose to interact with you. Continue to engage your faith and desire for more of God.

Engaging Faith and Desire Increases Your Ability to Hear God's Voice

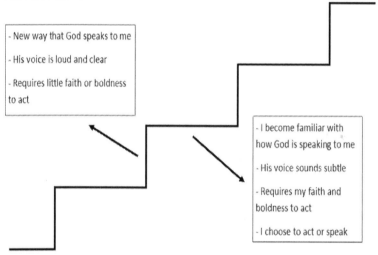

- New way that God speaks to me
- His voice is loud and clear
- Requires little faith or boldness to act

- I become familiar with how God is speaking to me
- His voice sounds subtle
- Requires my faith and boldness to act
- I choose to act or speak

Growing and maturing in hearing God's voice can follow a typical growth pattern. As you pursue your desire to hear God's voice, He will speak to you in different ways, and as a result, your sensitivity to His voice will improve. As mentioned before, your faith and desire play a key role in continuing to grow in hearing God's voice.

When God begins to speak to you in a new way that you are not familiar with, His voice will frequently sound loud and obvious. With time, you will naturally become familiar with the new way that He is speaking to you. This is usually when His voice becomes subtler and sounds more like your voice. The reason for this is because, at this point, His voice is becoming more and more at home in your heart. Do not entertain thoughts of doubt when He shifts to subtler methods of communicating. God's subtle voice is just as valid as His obvious or loud voice. Instead, continue to exercise your faith and believe that He wants to speak to you, and then engage your desire to draw close to Him in relationship. A helpful tip is to remember how it felt when He first began speaking in this new way with a more obvious voice. When His voice becomes more familiar, it will feel similar, just be subtler.

<u>Entertaining Doubt Stifles Your Ability to Hear God's Voice</u>

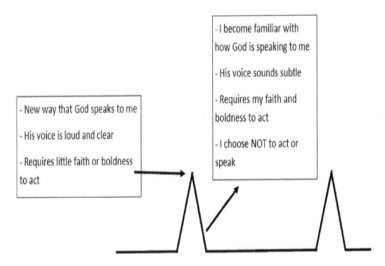

The truths contained in the following Scriptures are for <u>you</u>. These verses emphasize relationship and communication between you and Father God, Jesus, and Holy Spirit.

"No eye has seen, no ear has heard, and no mind has imagined what God has prepared for those who love him." But it was to us that God revealed these things by his Spirit. For his Spirit searches out everything and shows us God's deep secrets. (1 Corinthians 2:9-10)

"My sheep listen to my voice; I know them, and they follow me." (John 10:27)

"I no longer call you servants, because a servant does not know his master's business. Instead, I have called you friends, for everything that I learned from my Father I have made known to you." (John 15:15, NIV)

Doubt is a tactic that Satan employs to disrupt your communion with God. He will try everything in his power to sow thoughts of doubt to persuade you to believe that you can't hear God's voice, that God doesn't want to speak to you, or that you are doing it wrong. He will do his utmost to try and keep you from developing your sensitivity to hearing God's voice and deepening your relationship with Him. The truth is that, as a child of God, you *can* hear His voice, and He calls you friend. Friendship involves two-way communication.

If you only speak or act when God's voice is loud and clear and when you know for sure that it is Him, you will miss out on all the subtle times that He speaks and the depth of relationship that can develop as result. Learn how to hear the gentle whisper of God. God knows the best way for you to receive information from Him and for what purpose, so it is important to be open to all the ways that He desires to make His voice known.

Learning to hear God's voice is like an art. Your listening improves and is refined with practice. The following are some tips that can help you fine-tune and practice your listening skills:

Tips for How to Continue to Grow in Hearing God's Voice

Find at least one dominant way that God speaks to you

Everyone has at least one way that they hear, sense, or perceive God's voice. Learning to hear God's voice is like tuning into a favourite radio station on a radio: you listen for the announcer that you know and the songs that they play. Like the familiar radio station, Father God, Jesus, Holy Spirit, and the Bible are familiar to you. Listen for their voice and the essence of who they are. When you are able to target one way that God speaks to you, you can then actively commune with God through this avenue.

Biblical community is valuable in helping you recognize how you are hearing from God. When you become so accustomed to how God personally speaks to you that you think it's your own voice, those in biblical community with you can help highlight and confirm the voice of God in your life. Specifically, as you speak to others about what you are sensing God is saying, ask them for feedback. In a similar fashion, when someone speaks to you and you feel the truth of God speaking through him or her, tell that person! This will help that other individual pinpoint how God personally speaks to them as well.

<u>Learn how others hear from God</u>

As you practice listening to God, pay attention to how others receive their information from God. As you learn the variety of ways that God speaks to His people, it will increase your awareness of the possibilities of how He may want to speak to you in the future. Sometimes, all God needs is an openness to begin communicating in a different way. Commune with God in the way you know best, but desire and pursue other ways for Him to speak to you as well.

Hopefully, you are journeying with at least one friend as you engage in your own Deeper journey with God. This will make it easier to discover different ways that God speaks that may be unfamiliar to you. Witnessing and hearing how others hear from God will open your spirit up to potential ways that God may use to communicate with you as you learn and grow in hearing His voice.

<u>Journal what you are hearing, sensing, and perceiving from God</u>

Write down what you sense the Lord saying to you even outside of the formal, *Deeper* listening exercises. Journaling captures the details. Remember that there will be times when you are listening where it may not be clear in the moment if it is God speaking, or if it is your own thoughts and internal voice. Time may be required to grow the 'fruit' – that which proves it is God's voice. Journaling makes it easier to revisit past listening times to confirm or not that what you thought you heard was, indeed, His voice.

Act when you sense the Lord is asking you to do or say something

Taking action is often the only way that you will know if what you've heard is from God or not. Be willing to act and take risks. This will most likely require faith and boldness; it is a choice! Be faithful to steward what the Lord is giving you, and He will continue to give you more.

Look for supernatural fruit as evidence that God has spoken to you

As you hear God's voice and follow the principles of Deeper (lining up what you hear with the Bible and God's character), then you should be left with words that will encourage you, edify you, and comfort you. At the very least, you have encouraged yourself in 100% of your power. If it was your voice that you heard, then you have done exactly what the Bible asks us to do: *"...encourage one another and build each other up..."* (1 Thessalonians 5:11) You just happen to be the 'one another'!

You may be wondering if the words you heard were from within yourself or from God. If this is the case, look for specific fruit. We have all felt the fruit of human encouragement: we were uplifted, inspired, and motivated. If the words you heard were from God, however, you will experience *supernatural* fruit in the words:

- Truth and life – Jesus is called truth and life. (John 14:6)
- Love – God is love. (1 John 4:8)
- Freedom – The Spirit of God releases freedom. (2 Corinthians 3:17)

168

- Joy, peace, patience, kindness, goodness, faithfulness, gentleness, self-control – The fruit of Holy Spirit. (Galatians 5:22-23)
- Wisdom that is: pure, peace loving, gentle, willing to yield, full of mercy. (James 3:17)
- You are spiritually and positively changed in the interaction. (2 Corinthians 3:18)
- You are shown things that there is no way that you could have known about except through divine revelation – God conceals things, and I have the privilege to discover them. (Proverbs 25:2)

Supernatural fruit comes from Father God, Jesus, and Holy Spirit. This kind of fruit impacts you at a level that human words cannot. It goes 'deeper'. Some of this supernatural fruit becomes evident even as the words are spoken out, but other times, the fruit needs time to grow. If any of this fruit manifests in the words that you are hearing or appears as time goes on, then it is, in fact, God speaking to you! You are on the right path! Keep pressing on in your relationship with God and your listening in faith!

If hearing God's voice is not coming easily for you, keep practicing. Don't become discouraged! Remember that the Bible is the primary way that God speaks to His children. Even if the Bible is the only way that God speaks to you, that is enough!

Listening Exercise

A Place to 'Come Away'

Just as Jesus would regularly leave the crowd and His disciples to spend time with His Father, so should we make this a rhythm in our lives. Our listening exercise today will help you in meeting with a member of the Trinity in a special place of their choosing. Either listen in the way that you have found is the most natural or begin this exercise by engaging God in vision through your imagination.

Prepare yourself to abide in Jesus. You may find it helpful to listen to the song "Come Away" by Jesus Culture as a lead in to this listening activity. Then, pray the following prayer to prepare yourself to hear God's voice:

"In the name of Jesus, I silence the voice of any spirits that are contrary to Holy Spirit. I joyfully submit my spirit, soul, imagination, and body to You, Holy Spirit. I welcome You, Holy Spirit, to speak to me. I declare that I am God's child, and I hear His voice."

As you come before the Trinity with an open heart and spirit, activate your faith and trust, believing that the first thing that you see, hear, or sense is from God, and then ask more questions. Remember when you are done listening to line up what you have received with the Bible and the character of God.

Ask the following questions and journal the responses:

- Which member of the Trinity is going to meet with me?
- Where is a secret place (real or imaginary) for us to meet?

- Why did You pick this place?
- What do You want to say to me in this place You have chosen for us?

NOTE: If you are having difficulty engaging with a specific meeting place, picture with your imagination the cross of Jesus and use this as a starting place for Holy Spirit to add to.

Going Deeper
Extra Practice

Engage with Father God, Jesus, or Holy Spirit again and go back to your meeting place. Enter a fellowship of communion with the different members of the Trinity here. What else do they want to show you or speak to you about? Ask them questions about yourself in this place. Here are some ideas:

- What do You love about me? Why?
- What is something about me that makes You smile? Why?
- Where do You see that I am strong?
- Where do You see that I am weak?
- You promise that, in my weakness, You are strong. What is a strong part of You that You want to give me to cover my weakness?

Now that you have a meeting place with Father God, Jesus, or Holy Spirit, you can go back there at any time to commune with them, talk to them, etc. This is your special meeting place. Come away often!

Supernatural Exchange

Original painting by Deanna Oelke

Jesus gave me *"beauty for ashes, the oil of joy for mourning, the garment of praise for the spirit of heaviness..."* (Isaiah 61:3, NKJV)

Jesus had been speaking to me through this verse from Isaiah. I was coming out of a difficult season, and I could hear Jesus beckoning me to come to Him. I was so used to coming to Jesus with passion and exuberant worship that to come to Jesus with ashes, mourning, and heaviness seemed like such a pathetic offering. I hesitated. He promised me that, as I give my ashes to Him, He would supernaturally exchange them for beauty, oil of joy, and a garment of praise. Jesus only asks me to come and offer to Him what I have. When I do, my offering is transformed into something beautiful.

Chapter 8

Stewarding Truth

As you are listening to Holy Spirit, His spoken words of truth may just be the beginning of the journey that He has for you. Walking with Holy Spirit into deeper relationship with Father and Jesus is not just about listening. There is a parallel work of sanctification, healing, and restoration that He desires to accomplish.

Holy Spirit speaks words of truth that bring about life, love, and freedom. These words confront the lies of Satan, which produce fear, bondage, and death. By stewarding the truth that is spoken into your life, you can combat the lies of the enemy and defeat him.

When you hear words of living truth from Holy Spirit, you may find yourself having an emotional response – you may cry or feel like you could cry, or you may have another strong feeling bubble up from inside. Emotional responses are common when truth and words of life are spoken. You may not even understand why you are having this type of reaction. This could be a work that Holy Spirit is doing at a spirit level that has not yet been brought to your mind and understanding.

Pay attention to how you respond to Holy Spirit's truth that He directly speaks to you or that you receive from others through prophetic words. Do you feel relief, healing, a deep peace, hope, excitement, or some other response? Be aware that Holy Spirit's truth may be ending a work that He has been doing in your life, or His spoken truth is just the beginning of a new work that He wants to do in you. It is important to know how to steward truth and allow Holy Spirit to do the work that He desires.

Embrace the Sanctification Process

"Sanctify them by the truth; your word is truth." (John 17:17, NIV)

Truth is used by God to sanctify – to consecrate, make holy, cleanse, and unburden – His people. When you have a response to truth, it is important to embrace this process and begin to communicate with Holy Spirit. Try interacting with Him using the following questions:

- Is there anything else You want to say to me?
- Is this truth a finishing work, or is it the beginning of a new work You want to do?
- Do You simply want me to feel my feelings in Your presence and posture myself to receive from You?

Sometimes, all that Holy Spirit is asking is for us to submit, rest, and receive from Him. If you sense that Holy

Spirit wants to do a work at a spirit level, clear some time in your day to consciously engage with Him. Play worship music quietly in the background if you like. Position yourself to abide in Jesus (saying "yes" with your spirit, soul, and body) and allow Holy Spirit to do a transformational work within you. He may give you understanding up front as to what He is doing (a healing, a restoration, etc.), or He may desire that you simply trust Him with the process and just receive from Him.

Next, explore with Holy Spirit the reasons behind the work He wants to do in your life. What area or situation is He speaking into? The following are a few specifics that He may want to speak truth into:

Is there a wound that needs to be healed?

Occasionally, pain is the initial feeling you may experience when Holy Spirit speaks into your life. Pain is a common response to something within your being that needs healing. It highlights an area that God wants to work on. Therefore, we each have two choices as to how we respond to the pain.

- Ignore it and push it aside. Please realize that, if this is your response and Holy Spirit desires to bring healing, it *will* come up again in the future.
- Take your pain to Jesus. Choose to trust Him. Ask Jesus to lead you into healing and wholeness. He knows the perfect process for you to receive healing from the Great Physician.

Is there a character issue within me that needs to be dealt with?

The Lord disciplines those He loves (Hebrews 12:6). Be quick to submit and say "yes" to the work that Holy Spirit wants to do, and then do your part in cooperating with Him. When God is working on a character issue in our lives, it involves submission to Jesus, discipline, and good choices on our part. As your ability to hear God's voice grows, desire holiness. Holy Spirit will be quick to honour this desire, as this is also His heart for you.

Is there a lie that I have believed that needs to be replaced by truth?

Addressing this will be the focus of our teaching in *Deeper* in this chapter. This is a critical area to deal with because truth comes up against the lies of Satan. In this confrontation, a lie is exposed and needs to be replaced by God's truth.

Whatever Holy Spirit wants to do, allow Him to complete the work that He has started. Remember, there is no condemnation for those who are in Christ Jesus. As lies of the enemy, character issues, wounds, etc. bubble to the surface, be quick to run to Jesus for His sanctifying work to be accomplished in your life. You are never disqualified from being God's child. He will always love you. He knows all the issues that are in your life that need to be dealt with. Trust Holy Spirit and His timing in bringing issues to your attention. His timing is perfect for you.

My Identity

Often truth that Holy Spirit speaks to you is related to and impacts your identity. Your identity is formed by your views and your beliefs about:

- Your relationship with the Holy Trinity
- Who you are in Jesus Christ
- Who you are created to be

My Relationship with the Trinity

Truth: I am a son/daughter of God

"For you are all children of God through faith in Christ Jesus." (Galatians 3:26)

"And you must love the Lord your God with all your heart, all your soul, and all your strength." (Deuteronomy 6:5)

Our first and greatest commandment is to love the Lord our God with all our heart, soul, and strength[11] and is all about our relationship with Father God, Jesus, and Holy Spirit. As you journey deeper with the Holy Trinity, Satan will try to slow your journey, interfere with your relationships, and attempt to sow lies about the Triune God. Satan is called the father of lies (John 8:44). As lying is one of his biggest strategies, his lies are often attached to wounds, experiences, or our feelings. Hurtful experiences especially can make lies easier to believe.

---

[11] (Matthew 22:37)

Who I Am in Jesus Christ

Truth: I am a new person in Jesus Christ

> *"This means that anyone who belongs to Christ has become a new person. The old life is gone; a new life has begun!"* (2 Corinthians 5:17)

> *"What counts is whether we have been transformed into a new creation. May God's peace and mercy be upon all who live by this principle; they are the new people of God."* (Galatians 6:15b-16)

At times, the words that Holy Spirit speaks to us will be directly related to this foundational truth: I am a new person in Jesus Christ. However, Satan wants to keep us from fully knowing who we are in Jesus; he wants us to relate to our old, dead nature. Satan lies to us about who we are to keep us from living as a new person in the power of our Saviour. Our identity and who we are in Jesus Christ is vitally important to living in the fullness and the freedom of true Christianity.

I want to detail one of the most beautiful visions that I have ever had as it illustrates this principle of who we are in Jesus Christ. I received it from the Lord as I was beginning to step into my season of restoration and was experiencing an increase in my ability to hear from God.

I was at church on a Sunday morning, and it was Communion time. With an open Communion table, we were to come to the front and take Communion when we were ready. I took the bread and the wine, knelt at the front, and closed my eyes to prepare my heart to partake. I instantly saw in my imagination that I was standing on a dance floor. The dance floor was lit with a spotlight. This image on my imagination was random and was not anything that I was thinking about in the natural. I instantly took a posture of abiding and pressed my spirit into the Spirit of God for more. As the image continued, it was like I was watching a movie.

I saw Jesus step out of the shadows into the spotlight and walk toward me. His whole being emanated joy – His eyes twinkled, and He had a huge smile on His face. He approached me, and then we began to dance.

After watching us dance for a while, I took the bread and then prepared to take the wine. Before I took the wine, Jesus told me to bless it. Blessing it, I then closed my eyes and drank the wine. As I drank the wine, I saw it spiritually become Jesus' blood and begin to move throughout my entire body. I felt Jesus saying that He was covering me with His blood on the inside of me. As He said this and the blood moved to the extremities of my body, Jesus showed me that He was covering me with Himself on the outside of my body. There was an invisible Jesus completely over me and around me. I was completely in Jesus.

Then, I saw with my imagination that I was on the dance floor once again. This time, God the Father approached me to dance with me. He was more serious than Jesus, yet love shone out of His eyes. Father and I could dance together because I was covered in Jesus and thus completely holy and righteous.

When we danced close to the edges of the dance floor, I could see a dark figure standing in the shadows, arms crossed and scowling. It was Satan, and he was angry because he knew he could not touch me because I was in Jesus Christ. God the Father threw His head back and laughed because He knew that I was safe and protected.

This vision had so many spiritual truths illustrated in it. As I have shared it with others over the years, I have realized that this vision is not just for me, but it is for everyone in Jesus. This is God's desire for each of us: to live in the completeness of who we are in Jesus Christ where Satan cannot touch us.

Being Who I was Created to Be

Truth: I am fearfully and wonderfully made

"I praise you because I am fearfully and wonderfully made; your works are wonderful, I know that full well." (Psalm 139:14, NIV)

As you engage in relationship with God and live in who you are in Jesus Christ, you will discover who you were created to be: unique and wonderful! Throughout this relationship journey, Holy Spirit will show you details about yourself that He loves. As you learn more about yourself and embrace who God created you to be, you will develop a healthy, godly self-love and praise Him for the way that He made you! You can then live in the fullness of your gifting, personality, and uniqueness.

Satan would want you to believe that loving the way God made you will foster pride. This thinking will cause you to shrink back from fully embracing who you were created to be. If you are concerned about falling into pride, ask Holy Spirit to show you when you have had a prideful attitude. He will honour this prayer and show you how to adjust your mindset to stay humble before Him yet still be the person you were created to be with boldness and confidence.

I am so thankful in my healing journey that one of the first character issues that God worked on in my life was pride. After my deliverance and as God began to restore me, I discovered that God created me to be a confident person. I also discovered that He created me for significance and a desire to have an impact on people. I also love talking in front of large groups. When I first recognized some of the unique gifts and strong personality traits that God had created within me, my tendency was to shrink back as I was concerned about stepping into pride again. Satan used this opportunity to sow a lie: *"Desiring to have a large impact on a large group of people and enjoying speaking in front of people is prideful. You are full of pride."* As I expressed my enjoyment of speaking and having a microphone in hand, I would even have people say to me, "That is prideful." Again, I would shrink back. In my healing and restoration, I needed God's perspective of what true pride is.

Holy Spirit kindly brought me to repentance for believing the lie of Satan by revealing that I was created to be a leader. For that reason, I needed certain gifts and character traits to do what I was called to do. How He wanted me to lead was from a stage to maximize my impact for the sake of God's Kingdom. I honestly wondered, however, how I would journey in the *fullness* of how I was created – having that boldness and confidence as well as a love of speaking before a crowd – without stepping into pride. Holy Spirit helped me in my thinking around this.

My desire is to live my life here on earth in the largest way possible, having the most impact in God's Kingdom that I can. I desire to live in all of the fullness of who God has created me to be. No matter how showy or confident it looks, I yearn to step into all the opportunities that He intends for me to partake of, so that when I die and stand before my Father in Heaven, I can throw my life crown down as an offering at His feet and say, "You are so worthy to receive all my praise!"

Whenever I have opportunities that I feel have the potential to foster pride, I ask myself, *"Could I lay this at the Lord's feet right now?"* If I am tempted to hold onto the 'crown', then I know that there is a work that Holy Spirit needs to do in my heart, and I submit to Him. If I feel I can lay the 'crown' at the feet of Jesus, then I know that I am not operating in pride, and I embrace the fullness of the opportunity that God desires for me.

Using Truth to Replace Lies

When you find yourself reacting to the truth that Holy Spirit has spoken to you and you subsequently realize you have believed a lie that is contrary to the truth of the Bible, you can step into freedom from that lie in the following way. Remember, God knows what you are thinking, but Satan does not. When you are stepping out of the hold that Satan has had on you (like believing a lie), make sure you speak out loud. Let Satan hear that he is losing the power of the lie over you.

How to Break the Hold of a Lie

- What is the lie that you have believed?
  - Example: "I am prideful; I will always be prideful."
- Repent out loud for believing this lie.
  - Example: "Jesus, forgive me for believing that I am and will always be prideful."
- Replace the lie with truth. This may be truth revealed by Holy Spirit to you directly, or it may simply be finding a Scripture that combats the lie that you have believed. Declare out loud who you are in Jesus Christ.

o   Example: "Thank you, Jesus, that as a new person in You, I am righteous and holy (Ephesians 4:24). Therefore, in You, I am free from pride and can receive Your character of humility."

• Declare out loud: "In the name of Jesus, I silence the voice of the enemy in speaking this lie over me."

Fighting with Truth

Now that lies have been replaced with truth, use it as the sword of the Spirit. Fight with it! Receiving truth to replace lies is just the start of walking into victory. You now need to *live* in the truth. Do not allow Satan to steal this truth from you. As you walk in truth, you will be walking in new victory.

Strategies:

• Write out the truth and corresponding Bible verses that were given to you by Jesus, Holy Spirit, or Father God. Put them somewhere where you will see them on a regular basis.
• Memorize the Bible verses.
• Meditate on the Bible verses.
• Declare the truth out loud. You need to hear it, and Satan needs to be reminded of what you are choosing to believe. Declaring the Word of God out loud is spiritual warfare.
• Take every thought captive to the obedience of Christ (2 Corinthians 10:4-5). As thoughts come into your mind, ensure that they line up with the truth of God's Word. If thoughts are not lining up with truth, these may be lies that Satan is trying to have you own for yourself and then believe. If this happens, speak out,

"No, this is a lie. Be quiet in the name of Jesus!" and then speak truth out loud.

- As you are learning to live with new truth, Holy Spirit may show you behaviours that need to change. Trust His timing and His ways and be quick to change as He brings understanding and revelation to your heart.

As you journey deeper with the Holy Trinity, you will continue to spiritually grow and change. Sometimes, growth and changes are exciting. Still, there are other times when they are painful. During those moments when you are tempted to shrink back from the pain, ask yourself: *"Do I trust Jesus?"* God's heart is for you to live in the fullness of who He created you to be. Jesus desires you to live in the fullness of who you are in Him. And Holy Spirit is willing and more than able to journey with you and empower you to operate in that fullness! The Christian faith walk provides such an amazing opportunity to develop a beautiful relationship with the Trinity while discovering who we truly are in Jesus: healed, whole, delivered, and free!

"I pray that from his glorious, unlimited resources he will empower you with inner strength through his Spirit. Then Christ will make his home in your hearts as you trust in him. Your roots will grow down into God's love and keep you strong. And may you have the power to understand, as all God's people should, how wide, how long, how high, and how deep his love is." (Ephesians 3:16-18)

Listening Exercise

Targeting Lies

The following listening exercise will help you target lies that you have believed, specifically about your relationship with Father God, Jesus, and Holy Spirit. This exercise will prepare your heart and spirit to receive any inner healing that needs to occur.

Come before the Lord in prayer to prepare yourself to hear God's voice. Remember to write down the first impression or thought that you have as you are listening. When you are done listening and journaling, then go back and make sure that what you have written lines up with the Bible and God's character.

Think about Jesus in a spiritual way:

- Ask Jesus if there is a lie that you have believed about Him specifically.
- Ask Jesus to show you when you first believed this lie.
- If a situation is brought to mind, forgive people as necessary. Repent if there is any way that you have sinned in the situation.
- Repent for believing the lie and renounce the lie out loud.
- Ask Jesus for truth related to the situation as well as for a truth statement you can use to specifically combat the lie you have believed.
- Ask Jesus if there is anything else that He would want to say to you.

Think about Holy Spirit in a spiritual way:

- Ask Holy Spirit if there is a lie that you have believed about Him specifically.
- Ask Holy Spirit to show you when you first believed this lie.
- If a situation is brought to mind, forgive people as necessary. Repent if there is any way that you have sinned in the situation.
- Repent for believing the lie and renounce the lie out loud.
- Ask Holy Spirit for truth related to the situation as well as for a truth statement you can use to specifically combat the lie you have believed.
- Ask Holy Spirit if there is anything else that He would want to say to you.

Think about Father God in a spiritual way:

- Ask Father if there is a lie that you have believed about Him specifically.
- Ask Father to show you when you first believed this lie.
- If a situation is brought to mind, forgive people as necessary. Repent if there is any way that you have sinned in the situation.
- Repent for believing the lie and renounce the lie out loud.
- Ask Father for truth related to the situation as well as for a truth statement you can use to specifically combat the lie you have believed.
- Ask Father if there is anything else that He would want to say to you.

Walk through this process to step into truth whenever you discover that you have believed a lie about one of the members of the Trinity. Satan is called the father of lies, and he is good at weaving lies into situations in our life to specifically target our relationship with God. As believers, it is our job to resist those lies. We do that by stewarding the truth of God wisely.

Going Deeper

Extra Practice

The following are truth statements. Meditate on these statements and the Bible verses that support and confirm these truths. Ask Holy Spirit which statements He would like to highlight to you. When He highlights a verse or identity statement, write it out on a card and place it somewhere you will regularly see it to remind yourself of this truth. Asking questions, journey with Him to discover the fullness of who you truly are.

<u>Who I am in Jesus Christ</u>

- As a disciple, I am a friend of Jesus Christ. (John 15:15)
- I have been given the mind of Christ. (1 Corinthians 2:16)
- I am free forever from condemnation. Romans 8:1
- I may approach God with freedom and confidence. (Ephesians 3:12)
- I have been raised up and seated with Christ in Heaven. (Ephesians 2:6)

- I am an alien and stranger to this world that I temporarily live in. (1 Peter 2:11)
- I am hidden with Christ in God. (Colossians 3:1-4)
- I am chosen of God, holy, and dearly loved. (Colossians 3:12)
- I am righteous and holy. (Ephesians 4:24)
- I am God's child. (John 1:12)
- I have been redeemed and forgiven of all my sins. (Colossians 1:13-14)
- I am free from any condemnation brought against me, and I cannot be separated from the love of God. (Romans 8:31-39)
- I have been given the Holy Spirit as a pledge guaranteeing my inheritance to come. (Ephesians 1:13-14)
- I am a citizen of Heaven. (Philippians 3:20)
- I have not been given a spirit of fear but of power, love, and a sound mind. (2 Timothy 1:7)
- I have been justified – completely forgiven and made righteous. (Romans 5:1)
- I have been chosen by God and adopted as His child. (Ephesians 1:3-8)
- I am a member of Christ's body. (1 Corinthians 12:27)
- I am a son/daughter of light and not of darkness. (1 Thessalonians 5:5)
- I am united with the Lord, and I am one with Him in spirit. (1 Corinthians 6:17)
- I have been bought with a price, and I belong to God. (1 Corinthians 6:19-20)
- I am complete in Christ. (Colossians 2:9-10)
- I am God's workmanship. (Ephesians 2:10)
- I am born of God, and the evil one cannot touch me. (1 John 5:18)

- I am assured that God works for my good in all circumstances. (Romans 8:28)
- I have been crucified with Christ, and it is no longer I who live but Christ who lives in me. (Galatians 2:20)
- I have direct access to the throne of grace through Jesus Christ. (Hebrews 4:14-16)
- I can do all things through Christ who strengthens me. (Philippians 4:13)
- I am a chosen race, a royal priesthood, a holy nation, a people for God's own possession to proclaim the excellencies of Him. (1 Peter 2:9-10)
- I am not the great "I Am", but by the grace of God, I am what I am. (Exodus 3:14; John 8:24, 25, 28; 1 Corinthians 15:10)

Power, Authority, & Love

Original painting by Deanna Oelke

"And may you have the power to understand, as all God's people should, how wide, how long, how high, and how deep his love is. May you experience the love of Christ, though it is too great to understand fully. Then you will be made complete with all the fullness of life and power that comes from God."
(Ephesians 3:18-19)

To me, horses represent power and authority. When I finished painting this horse, his body and his eyes looked so gentle to me. I did not comprehend how the concept of power and authority could also possess the essence of gentleness. After I came across this passage from Ephesians, I finally understood. No one can stand against God's power and authority...yet He is also the embodiment of love. His love carries the essence of who He is: gentle.

193

Chapter 9

Dreams

I have always been a dreamer even as a young girl. Dreams have been another one of the predominant ways through which God has spoken to me. Therefore, I recognized the potential for God to do amazing things through my dreams. As I learned to hear God's voice and became more aware of the different avenues that He could use to speak to me, I specifically asked God for more dreams. He answered my desire by increasing my dreams.

Not all my dreams were from God, nor could I interpret them all. However, there were significant dreams that God used to speak to me in deep and profound ways. Holy Spirit and my prophetic friends were instrumental during this time in helping me learn how to interpret dreams for myself as well as for others.

As I search out the meaning of dreams, I press into Holy Spirit for the correct interpretation. There are times when I know right away what the interpretation is, whereas there are other times where I am not as confident in the dream's meaning or simply have no idea. I have found that God will occasionally withhold the meaning of a dream that I have dreamt and give it to someone in my faith community instead. This causes me to be interdependent on my faith community and continue to risk and share with them.

Early in my prophetic journey, God gave me healing dreams that ministered healing to parts of my soul. After I came back from the prophetic conference experience in Washington State, God began to heal my emotions regarding my love connection with Jesus. As a result, I would have dreams about Jesus. I would wake up from these dreams and feel an intense love for Jesus and feel the intensity of His love envelop me in return. After numerous dreams like this, I could then, during the day, continue to feel love for Jesus and His love for me. This was the first time in my life that I could engage in my relationship with Jesus and Father God motivated by love and not simply by choosing faith. I remember saying to my friends, "Living a Christian life is so much easier when you feel the love of Jesus!" I felt like Jesus' love was the oil in my engine of life; everything just ran more smoothly.

My daughter, Janessa, often has dreams that later happen. As she talks about her day, we frequently hear, "Oh, yeah, I dreamt about that." One time, she had a dream where she was at school with a friend, and the friend got hurt. In the dream, she felt the prompting of Holy Spirit to pray for her friend. However, she did not pray and then regretted that she did not obey. Sometime later, Janessa was at school and realized that she was living out exactly what she had dreamt. After her friend was hurt, Janessa remembered in the dream that she had regretted not praying for her friend. With this in mind, she made sure that she *did* pray for her friend. God had shown her in her dream how He wanted her to respond!

Dreams are often more symbolic than literal in nature. Therefore, it can be useful to learn about different dream symbols. The tendency here can be to rely completely on dream symbols to interpret dreams. This is where relying on Holy Spirit to give the interpretation is so vital to avoid a 'plug and play' mentality where you trust in the 'formula' versus the true source of wisdom.

If you are interested in learning more about dreams and dream interpretation, there is an excellent course from John Paul Jackson called "Understanding Dreams and Visions". This course can be taken online from the website for Streams Ministries.

Dreams in the Bible

"For God may speak in one way, or in another, yet man does not perceive it. In a dream, in a vision of the night, when deep sleep falls upon men, while slumbering on their beds, then He opens the ears of men, and seals their instruction." (Job 33:14-16, NKJV)

"And afterward, I will pour out my Spirit on all people. Your sons and daughters will prophesy, your old men will dream dreams, your young men will see visions." (Joel 2:28, NIV)

Dreams in the Bible were considered a legitimate way that God speaks. The following are some of the people that God spoke to through dreams in the Bible:

- Jacob (Genesis 28:12, 31:10)
- Laban (Genesis 31:24)
- Joseph (Genesis 37:5, 9)
- The butler and the baker (Genesis 40:5)
- Pharaoh (Genesis 41:1, 5)
- A man in the Midianite army (Judges 7:13)
- Solomon (1 Kings 3:5)
- Nebuchadnezzar (Daniel 2:3, 4:5)
- Daniel (Daniel 7:1)
- Joseph (Matthew 1:20, 2:13, 19, 22)
- The wise men (Matthew 2:12)
- Pilate's wife (Matthew 27:19)

There are only two known dream interpreters in the Bible: Joseph and Daniel. They both stated that their ability to interpret dreams came from God. Their God-given ability far surpassed the abilities of other dream interpreters in their time that were not children of God. This is an important truth for us to remember as we take a biblical view of dream interpretation. Relying on God is key – He is the source for correct interpretation.

Dream interpretation has been dropped by the Western church and has been picked up by the New Age movement and the secular world. Both the New Age and the world do not have Holy Spirit to rely on in the interpretive process. Instead of being led by the Kingdom of Heaven, they are relying on interpretive models and symbolism that is led by the soul and man's ideas and perceptions. It is time that Christians take back the art of dream interpretation as we purpose to rely on Holy Spirit to lead us into all truth for the interpretation of dreams.

Before we go through a simple dream interpretation process, it is important to note that not all dreams are from God. Just like in your listening, we can also have dreams that originate either from God, Satan, or ourselves. As you begin to dream, pay attention to your dreams. Rely on Holy Spirit to help you sift through your dreams to discover which ones are from God.

A Simple Interpretative Process

Without God's help, we will not be able to understand dreams. It is more than just having the necessary tools to interpret them. Just because you are prophetic, does not mean you will necessarily be good at dream interpretation. Some people are better at dream interpretation than others. A great way to see if you can interpret dreams is to practice. Practice on yourself with your dreams as well as with others using their dreams.

As you practice interpreting dreams, remember to:

- Rely on Holy Spirit as your main source and guide
- Become familiar with some dream symbols or look up dream symbols
- Ask Holy Spirit for the meaning
- Talk to prophetic friends and gain their help in interpreting your dreams

Once you become more familiar with dream symbols, remember that someone else's ideas of what symbols mean should serve only a guide. Your ultimate symbol guide and interpreter is Holy Spirit.

Simple Dream Interpretation Steps

1. Dreams that we have can come from 3 sources: God, Satan, and ourselves. Do you immediately have a sense of the origin of your dream? If not, enquire of Holy Spirit as to where the dream comes from.

2. Begin to record dreams that you sense are significant and may be from God. Even if you don't understand them or are unable to interpret them initially, write them down so that Holy Spirit can bring understanding in His timing.

3. If you have frequent nightmares, begin to pray God's covering or pray the blood of Jesus to cover you and your dreams before you go to sleep. If you sense the dream is from Satan, ask God what He would want to speak into the dream. Imagine the dream again. This time, ask Jesus to walk with you through the dream. Watch what Jesus does and ask Him what insights He wants to give you at key points throughout the dream. In this way, you can 'flip' the dream as you walk through it with Jesus according to the truth of His Word.

   - Example: If you have a dream about your life involving destruction and turmoil, walk through the dream with Jesus in the truth of Jeremiah 29:11. Flip the dream by reimagining the destruction and turmoil being overcome by God's plans that will prosper, not harm you, and with plans that will give you hope and a future.

4. If you think the dream may be from God, meditate on and work through the following:

- Try to reduce the dream to its simplest form. If you could title the dream, what would you title it?
- Determine the focus of the dream. Ask: "Who is this dream about? Who, or what, is the center of attention?"
- What were your feelings in the dreams? Were they positive, negative, or neutral?
- What are some important symbols in the dream? Pay particular attention to the following:
  - Colours
  - Numbers
  - Names of people
    - Does the name represent an actual person such as someone you know personally? If yes, what does this person mean to you? What might this person represent?
    - Or, the person might not be the focus. It might be their name and the meaning of their name that holds significance. Look up the meaning of the name on baby name websites.

5. Look up the meaning of the main symbols of the dream. TehillahDreams.com is an excellent website which uses a variety of good, Christian resources for its dream symbols. This website also has a dream symbol search engine.

6. Rely on Holy Spirit to sense an accurate interpretation. Steward your dream interpretation in the same way you would in listening to the voice of God: line it up with the Bible and the character of God. Once you sense from Holy Spirit that you have an accurate dream interpretation, discern what your part is. Is there something now that God wants you to do? Is God

requiring action on your part? Continue to press in to Holy Spirit to find out what is next. If you perceive that you don't have an accurate interpretation, lay the dream aside and come back to it when Holy Spirit leads you.

This whole dream interpretation process may take minutes, weeks, months, or sometimes years. Trust Holy Spirit and His leading as you pursue dream interpretation and endeavour to steward that interpretation.

I hope that you enjoy receiving and journeying with Holy Spirit in your dreams!

Listening Exercise
Dream Interpretation

Practice dream interpretation on your own dreams and with trusted friends and their dreams. If you find that you can do dream interpretation quite well, practice outside of your prophetic circle of friends. This is often an easy door to open as you initiate conversations with non-prophetic Christians and non-Christians alike since most people dream.

You can approach dream interpretation with others in the following way: "I have recently learned dream interpretation, and I was wondering if you would let me practice on you? Do you have a dream that I could try to interpret?" After walking through the dream interpretation process, ask them if they feel that this is accurate. Don't be afraid to say you don't know if you receive no interpretation from Holy Spirit.

Deeper – Part 2

Hearing God's Voice
for Others

Joel 2:28

Original painting by Deanna Oelke

"Then, after doing all those things, I will pour out my Spirit upon all people. Your sons and daughters will prophesy. Your old men will dream dreams, and your young men will see visions." (Joel 2:28)

I was praying one night when, instantly, I saw a vision of Father God holding a clay pot. As He tipped the pot, I saw water pouring out. The end of the water turned into a herd of galloping horses. Before I even had a chance to ask Him what this meant, I heard Him say, *"In the last days, I will pour my Spirit on all flesh."*

Holy Spirit is represented by the herd of horses. There is a sense of intensity, focus, and intentionality of Holy Spirit to carry out the will of Father God.

Chapter 10

What is the Gift of Prophecy?

At this point in the Deeper journey, we will be shifting from a focus of listening to God for ourselves to listening to God for others. You may find it helpful to read the next three chapters and then come back to practice the listening exercises at the end of each chapter. In doing so, you will then have all the information you need before practicing giving prophetic words.

The gift of prophecy simply defined is: listening to God for someone else and speaking out words that strengthen, encourage, and comfort the other person. All of the same principles and ways that you have learned to listen to God for yourself will be applied to listening to God for others. This is the practice of the gift of prophecy.

This gift from Holy Spirit truly does grow through practice. I encourage you to trust the voice of Holy Spirit that you have come to know as you have engaged with Him in the previous listening exercises. Furthermore, I encourage you to be obedient and bold in speaking out what you sense Holy Spirit is saying to you for others. Faithfully steward what He is giving you, and He will continue to give you more for the edification of others.

Up until this point, you may have been journeying through *Deeper* and learning how to hear God's voice on your own. For this next section, I encourage you to try and find someone to spiritually journey with and to practice giving prophetic words to. Ask Holy Spirit for someone who will be an 'iron sharpens iron' friend who will spur you on to love and good deeds (Hebrews 10:24). If you do not have someone to journey with, ask Holy Spirit to send you people who are open to receiving prophetic words so that you can actively utilize your gift of prophecy. Holy Spirit desires for you to grow in this gift, so trust His ways and the opportunities that He will give you to practice using your gift.

Hearing God's voice for yourself feels much safer and less risky than hearing God's voice for others and operating in the gift of prophecy. Sharing what you sense the Lord is saying with someone else requires more boldness on your part, which may seem scary. If you are staying within the guidelines of 1 Corinthians 14, plus your prophetic words are comforting, encouraging, and edifying, then at the very least, you are encouraging a person with 100% of your own power. God thinks that building others up in our own power is a good thing (1 Thessalonians 5:11). At the very most, your impressions will be from God, and the words you speak will be inspired by Him and thus supernaturally impact the other person in a way that no human encouragement can.

When you feel the witness of Holy Spirit and His gentle whisper, step out in faith, acting on it and speaking out what you are sensing. Also, watch and listen to how people respond to you as you prophesy to them. Are they emotional as you speak? Do they affirm that this is exactly what they needed to hear? Do they affirm that God was speaking through you? As these and other confirming responses occur, be encouraged that you are operating in the gift of prophecy.

As we steward our gift of prophecy, it is important to know what the Bible says in the New Testament regarding the gift of prophecy. Let's focus on New Testament Bible verses to provide a good biblical foundation for the gift of prophecy.

Holy Spirit Gives the Gift of Prophecy

"A spiritual gift is given to each of us so we can help each other. To one person the Spirit gives the ability to give wise advice; to another the same Spirit gives a message of special knowledge. The same Spirit gives great faith to another, and to someone else the one Spirit gives the gift of healing. He gives one person the power to perform miracles, and another the ability to prophesy. He gives someone else the ability to discern whether a message is from the Spirit of God or from another spirit. Still another person is given the ability to speak in unknown languages, while another is given the ability to interpret what is being said. It is the one and only Spirit who distributes all these gifts. He alone decides which gift each person should have."

(1 Corinthians 12:7-11)

The gift of prophecy is one of the gifts given by Holy Spirit that is referenced in 1 Corinthians 12. This passage of Scripture states that Holy Spirit decides which gift each person should have. You may receive the gift of prophecy from Holy Spirit simply by Him releasing it to you and without asking for it. The posture on your part is one of being open and willing for Holy Spirit to give to you what He chooses from this list of gifts.

Our Desire Releases Spiritual Gifts

In 1 Corinthians 14, we read more specifically about the gift of prophecy.

We can receive the gift of prophecy by desire on our part:

> *"Let love be your highest goal! But you should also desire the special abilities the Spirit gives—especially the ability to prophesy."* (1 Corinthians 14:1)

Paul as a leader expresses his desire for the Corinthians:

> *"...I wish you could all prophesy."* (I Corinthians 14:5a)

Paul encourages the Corinthians to seek the gifts of Holy Spirit:

> *"...Since you are so eager to have the special abilities the Spirit gives, seek those that will strengthen the whole church."* (1 Corinthians 14:12b)

These verses capture the heart of Father God towards us. Even though 1 Corinthians 12 states that Holy Spirit alone decides who will receive His gifts, the passage in 1

Corinthians 14 indicates that desire on our part can also release the gifts of Holy Spirit to us! Would God, as a good father, ask us to desire the gifts from Holy Spirit and then not give them to us? Of course not! God *is* a good father, and He knows how to give good gifts (Matthew 7:11). Father's heart wants us to long for the gifts of Holy Spirit, and He specifically wants to release the gift of prophecy to us! He may simply be waiting for us to express our desire for it. Do you yearn to cooperate with Holy Spirit through the gift of prophecy to strengthen, encourage, and comfort others in your biblical community? Then, desire the gift of prophecy and choose to journey with Holy Spirit so that He can release it to you!

I received my gift of prophecy simply by continuously desiring it, praying for it, and seeking Holy Spirit's guidance. I did not receive the gift of prophecy all at once. It was imparted to me over time. Holy Spirit led me to great reading material (E.g. *Approaching the Heart of Prophecy* by Graham Cooke), and Holy Spirit encouraged me to speak out prophetic words to others in faith. As I would speak out what Holy Spirit gave me, people would affirm that the words were from God, or they would affirm that it was exactly what they needed to hear. People's responses confirmed that Holy Spirit was indeed speaking. As I was faithful to do my part and steward what Holy Spirit was giving me, He continued to give me more prophetic words for others. With practice, my gift of prophecy grew and was strengthened.

Remember that Holy Spirit is, first and foremost, concerned about relationship with you (Mark 12:29-30). In your journey of growing in your prophetic gift, ensure that you become dependent on the *person* of Holy Spirit and not on the process of how He speaks to you.

We discussed in earlier chapters that Holy Spirit yearns to speak to His people in a variety of ways. This is also true as you listen for prophetic words for others. Sometimes, He may give you a prophetic word for someone, and you know for sure that He is speaking to you. In times like these, little to no faith is required to deliver what He has given you. Other times, He may speak more subtly, and more faith on your part is required to speak out the prophetic word. Most often, Holy Spirit longs to grow your faith during these times. Trust Him in the different ways He chooses to impart prophetic words to you and take those risks in speaking what you are sensing from Holy Spirit.

The Gift of Prophecy is for Encouragement

The gift of prophecy strengthens, encourages, and comforts:

"But one who prophesies strengthens others, encourages them, and comforts them." (1 Corinthians 14:3)

Prophecy strengthens the entire church:

"...but one who speaks a word of prophecy strengthens the entire church. ...prophecy is greater than speaking in tongues ... so that the whole church will be strengthened." (1 Corinthians 14:4, 5)

What would it be like if your church or biblical community was known for being an encouraging place? What if people sought out your community when they needed to be strengthened and comforted? What a testimony this would be of God's children operating in the love of Father God! I believe that this is one of the reasons why God encourages us in the Bible to eagerly desire the spiritual gifts, especially the gift of prophecy (1 Corinthians 14:1).

The gift of prophecy strengthens the whole church. Multiple people are blessed by this one gift. Even though you personally will be blessed by having the gift of prophecy, your gift is not for your benefit. It is primarily for the benefit and uplifting of the Body of Christ (1 Corinthians 12:7, 14:22).

Paul makes it clear in 1 Corinthians 14 that prophecy is for strengthening, encouraging, and comforting other Christians. Therefore, prophecy is not to be used to point out sin, correct, or judge other believers. This is very important to remember when exercising the gift of prophecy.

Within biblical community, there *will* be times when correction is required and there's a need to walk people through dealing with their sin, all the while loving them despite their issues. Yet, none of this should be done through a spoken, prophetic word of God. Instead, if someone needs to be corrected or confronted in your biblical community, consider the following suggestions. First, make certain that you are in right relationship with the person before addressing them. Secondly, make sure you are following the prompting of Holy Spirit and obeying His direction regarding the matter. Finally, any correction should be delivered in love.

You don't have to be prophetic to see the sin or the issues in other people's lives. You *do* have to be prophetic to find the treasures deep within the hearts of people. Ask Holy Spirit to see the treasure. Be a treasure hunter!

Distinction Between the Logos Word and the Rhema Word of God

Logos Word of God:

"All Scripture is God-breathed and is useful for teaching, rebuking, correcting and training in righteousness, so that the servant of God may be thoroughly equipped for every good work." (2 Timothy 3:16-17, NIV)

Rhema Word of God:

"But the one who prophesies speaks to people for their strengthening, encouraging and comfort." (1 Corinthians 14:3, NIV)

These two verses give a clear distinction between the role of the Logos and Rhema Word of God. The Logos – the written Word of God – is for teaching, rebuking, correcting, and training in righteousness. The Rhema – the spoken Word of God or prophetic word – is for strengthening, encouraging, and comforting. Sometimes Holy Spirit might show you things about a person that may be the reality of where they spiritually are, and this reality may not be encouraging. When this happens, ask Holy Spirit how He sees them. He will show you what they look like healed, whole, and delivered in Jesus Christ. If you are unsure if your prophetic word is going to build the other person up, ask yourself, *"Would I want to receive this prophetic word for myself?"* If not, ask Holy Spirit to help you adjust it into a strengthening, encouraging, and comforting word.

When I receive a word that reveals and provides insight into the reality of where the other person is at and where

Holy Spirit shows me sin in their life, I do *not* speak this out to the person. They probably already know the sin that they are struggling with and would most likely be embarrassed if they knew that I knew, and they'd be even more embarrassed if I spoke it out in front of others. In a case like this, Holy Spirit is placing a great deal of trust in me to steward this information well. I take these situations very seriously and press in closely to Holy Spirit for His wisdom and the encouraging words that He desires me to speak.

For every sin that is in our lives, Holy Spirit has a plan of redemption, resolution, and restoration. *This* is what I ask Holy Spirit for upon receiving a word that is not initially strengthening, encouraging, and comforting, for *this* is what the person needs to hear! They need to hear the hope of who they are in Jesus Christ: free from their sin. Knowing the sin in someone's life gives me compassion and understanding with what they are facing. After I deliver a freedom, prophetic word – a word where Holy Spirit has taken a negative insight and turned it into a word that builds the other person up – I will often continue to pray for the person and their journey into freedom as Holy Spirit reminds me.

Prophesying Requires Us to Engage Faith

"We have different gifts, according to the grace given to each of us. If your gift is prophesying, then prophesy in accordance with your faith." (Romans 12:6, NIV)

Faith is confidence in what we hope for and assurance about what we do not see (Hebrews 11:1). As we prepare to prophesy to someone, we need to activate our faith and belief in the biblical principles behind the gift of prophecy. To exercise our faith with regard to prophecy, we must believe that God's heart is to talk to His people. We also need to engage our faith that Holy Spirit desires to cooperate with us to strengthen, encourage, and comfort others within the Body. Our choice is to have either a little faith in these principles or a lot of faith, for we then prophesy according to the level of faith we have.

As mentioned before, when I first began listening to God's voice and practiced giving prophetic words, God chose to speak to me in very subtle ways. For the majority of prophetic words that I received, they truly felt like they were my own thoughts, feelings, and imagination. This required a choice of boldness and faith on my part to believe that God was speaking to me and directing my words. As I spoke out each prophetic word, the people receiving those words confirmed that it was indeed Holy Spirit speaking to me. This validated that I was truly hearing from God but receiving the words did not become easier. I believe that God spoke softly with intention to increase my personal faith.

I have seen many people only speak out prophetic words when they are certain God is speaking. The caution in this is that you can miss the gentle whispers of God (1 Kings 19:12-13). Choose to step out in faith and speak out even the soft, gentle impressions that you receive, and then watch if people confirm that this is God speaking through you. The affirming feedback will help you tune into the subtle ways that God is using to speak to you.

We can all choose to have faith, but we can also ask for the spiritual gift of supernatural faith as stated in 1 Corinthians 12:9. When I first meditated on these gifts of Holy Spirit, I remember thinking that the gift of faith was a boring gift. I could not see the value of this gift since we all can choose to have faith. God must have smiled at my naivety. As I was growing in my prophetic gift, Holy Spirit decided one Christmas to give me the gift of supernatural faith. Instantaneously, I had faith in situations that I needed to previously choose to have faith. It was like my own faith but on steroids! Within a very short time, I could see how powerful this gift from Holy Spirit was. This gift of faith also helped me in prophesying. Not only did I prophesy in accordance with my faith, I now could prophesy in accordance with my gift of supernatural faith.

Prophesy in Love

"If I have the gift of prophecy and can fathom all mysteries and all knowledge, and if I have a faith that can move mountains, but do not have love, I am nothing." (1 Corinthians 13:2, NIV)

We are <u>nothing</u> without love. This is a strong statement. Love should be our goal as we prophesy...always. As you operate in your gift of prophecy, ask yourself, *"When people witness me using my prophetic gift, are they seeing and hearing the language of love?"* The more you learn to love God, the better you will be able to love yourself as well as love others (Mark 12:29-30). You prophesy from the place of what your relationship with Father God is like and what you know about His characteristics. The more we grow in our relationship with God and experience Him as Love, the better we will speak His language of love and release His nature of love.

If you find that you desire to give corrective, prophetic words or want to point out sin and what is wrong in the lives of others, question Holy Spirit as to why. If you believe that Father is an angry God, you will prophesy from this place of anger. The truth is that God is Love (1 John 4:17), and all the fruit of the Spirit is within God and available to us (Galatians 5:22-23). God's love and these fruits should be evident in our lives and come through in our prophetic words.

As I made my relationship with Father God, Jesus, and Holy Spirit my primary goal, and as I was learning to prophesy and operate in my gift, I began to see that my view of people changed. I am naturally a person that sees situations and people in black and white, and I can easily see things that people need to change and work on. As I learned to love the Lord with all my heart, soul, mind, and strength, I was changed in the process. When I would prophesy, it was like God gave me 'love glasses' to look through – I literally could see people as He saw them, and I experienced His immense love for them. Because I felt God's love for others, I began to have a natural love for them as well. The reality of 1 John 4:19 became my experience, for I was able to love because God first loved me. Since I had experienced the fullness of God's love toward me within my relationship with Him, I was able to more fully love others. One of the things that I love the most about my gift of prophecy is that, as I have pursued relationship with God and used my gift, I have been changed more and more into Jesus' likeness.

We Prophesy in Part

"Love never fails. But where there are prophecies, they will cease; where there are tongues, they will be stilled; where there is knowledge, it will pass away. For we know in part and we prophesy in part, but when completeness comes, what is in part disappears." (1 Corinthians 13:8-10, NIV)

218

Do not assume that when God shows you details and gives insight about a person that you see the whole picture. We prophesy in part and see only part of the whole. Be faithful to deliver the 'part' that you see, and God will work in the person to show them the 'whole' in His timing and in His way.

When we operate in the gift of prophecy and sense and see things about people, we need to remember this principle. It can be very easy to slip into the attitude of: *"I know better than you because I hear from God."* After God shows us things about people, we must be very careful to not judge them, especially when they make choices that are different than what we think is God's best. Remember that each Christian you prophesy over has Holy Spirit to guide them in their lives. Trust God to draw them to Himself through His Spirit, His Word, and through other believers. Our responsibility is simply to prophesy with love and then continue to love them in their journey.

God Values Order as We Prophesy

"Let two or three people prophesy, and let the others evaluate what is said. But if someone is prophesying and another person receives a revelation from the Lord, the one who is speaking must stop. In this way, all who prophesy will have a turn to speak, one after the other, so that everyone will learn and be encouraged. Remember that people who prophesy are in control of their spirit and can take turns. For God is not a God of disorder but of peace, as in all the meetings of God's holy people.

"So, my dear brothers and sisters, be eager to prophesy, and don't forbid speaking in tongues. But

be sure that everything is done properly and in order."
(1 Corinthians 14:29-33, 39-40)

This passage of Scripture shows that prophesying in a group should be done in an orderly way with everyone having a turn. At times, you may feel an urgency to deliver a prophetic word. Remember that God is patient, and love is also patient. Keep in mind that you are in control of your own spirit and thus can take turns prophesying with others.

God Asks Us to Submit to Our Leaders

"Have confidence in your leaders and submit to their authority, because they keep watch over you as those who must give an account. Do this so that their work will be a joy, not a burden, for that would be of no benefit to you." (Hebrews 13:17, NIV)

If you are giving prophetic words in your church, be diligent to submit to its leadership and follow their prophetic protocol. This ensures that you operate in your gift in a way that will be received by the leadership over you. Additionally, you also need to speak in a way that is accepted by the people within your church body. Be culturally relevant and use words that your biblical community will understand. In this way, you will be of benefit to all.

If your church leadership is not accepting of prophetic words, yet you desire to prophesy, you have two choices. You can either submit to their authority, not giving out any prophetic words within that community, or you can move to a church where prophetic words are readily received. If you believe it would be best to leave your church, first make certain that Holy Spirit is calling you to leave and that your heart is humble. Whatever choice you make, your heart and spirit must be in alignment with God's will.

Listening Exercise
Using Your Prophetic Gift

If you are hearing God for yourself on a regular basis, you truly will be able to hear God's voice for others. I hope that you have begun to speak out to friends and others in your biblical community as you sense that God is speaking to you a message of encouragement for them. If you are unsure if you have the gift of prophecy, begin to eagerly desire it and pray for Holy Spirit to release it to you!

The following listening exercise is meant to be done with another person, ideally someone who is on the Deeper journey with you. If you are not journeying with someone, ask a friend that knows you well if they would be willing to allow you to practice on them. You will then be the only one doing the prophesying, and your friend would just receive from you and then give you feedback.

Partner Prophesying

In pairs, ask the Lord the following questions for each other. The encouragement here is to speak what you are sensing from Holy Spirit without writing it down. Share one at a time the revelations that you receive. Provide feedback to each other.

1. Jesus, what colour is this person like? Why? What does that mean?
   (Share with each other)

2. Ask God to give you a Bible verse for the other person. Then, ask Him for one specific aspect, word, or part of the verse that He desires to particularly highlight. Next, seek Him for what He wants to tell the other person through it. Avoid preaching the Word. Instead, hear and deliver the personal message that is on God's heart right now for your partner.
(Share)

3. Request that God give you an inner picture or vision for your partner. Ask Him what He wants to reveal to them through it.
(Share)

4. Ask God to let you feel a certain emotion. Then, request that God show you what that emotion means for the other person and what exactly does He want to say or impart as a result.
(Share)

Psalm 91

Original painting by Deanna Oelke

"Whoever dwells in the shelter of the Most High will rest in the shadow of the Almighty." (Psalm 91:1, NIV)

I painted this flaming lion during worship one Sunday evening. He turned out so beautifully that I knew I wanted to repaint him and take more time. As I envisioned the details, I kept seeing a shadow of a woman dancing in the shadow of the lion. When I asked Jesus what that was, He told me, *"Psalm 91."* I found this very odd because I have always pictured Psalm 91 as very peaceful and serene. The Lord explained to me that the reason it is peaceful for me is because of what my enemy, Satan, sees. He sees Jesus – the roaring lion of Judah! As a result, Satan does not dare come near.

I painted the woman touching the flames because I always feel a certain amount of refining while I am in Psalm 91. This is because the Lord wants to burn away any foothold that Satan may have in my life so that Satan will have no hold on me.

Chapter 11

Old and New Covenant Prophecy

I find that as Christians begin learning about the gift of prophecy, they have many questions regarding how this gift differs from prophecy they have read about in the Old Testament. When they explore verses in the New Testament that emphasize the encouraging, non-judging nature of prophetic words, they often question why prophetic words in the Old Testament pointed out people's sin and judged the people. Prophecy and prophets were a prominent part of Old Testament life, and people have often assumed that the gift of prophecy will look like Old Testament prophecy.

Prophecy in the Old Testament is not a model for us to follow with our gift of prophecy. A significant shift happened in prophecy on the day of Pentecost when Holy Spirit was sent to dwell within all who believe in the name of Jesus (John 14:16-18). Because of Jesus' finishing work on the cross, fulfilling the law and the prophets, we can now step into New Covenant principles and New Covenant prophecy. Instead of making a distinction between Old and New Testament prophecy, I will be making a distinction between Old and New *Covenant* prophecy as the shift happened on the day of Pentecost.

Old and New Covenant

The Old Covenant was a physical, earth-based agreement that was initially made at Mount Sinai with the children of Israel. It required obedience to the letter of God's law. It promised that a person or a nation would be physically blessed (health, wealth, etc.) or cursed (poverty, captivity, etc.) depending on whether or not they obeyed all of God's written commandments and statutes.

The New Covenant, in contrast to the Old, is spiritually based. It is centered on obedience from the heart and a fulfilling of God's laws, not only in the letter, but also in their spiritual intent. It promises an eternal life full of love and glory for those who ask Jesus to be the Lord and Saviour of their lives and eternal death for those who do not receive Him. In the Sermon on the Mount[12], Jesus issues the beginning words of the New Covenant.

---

[12] (Matthew 5, 6, 7)

Old Covenant

"Indeed, there is no one on earth who is righteous, no one who does what is right and never sins." (Ecclesiastes 7:20, NIV)

Old Testament prophets reminded people of their sin in falling short of God's standard and that they could not perfectly follow the law. They continuously pointed out that the Old Covenant was failing. This led to Old Covenant prophets highlighting the people's desperate need for a Saviour, and they pointed to Jesus and prophesied His coming.

Jesus fulfilled the Old Covenant

"Do not think that I [Jesus] have come to abolish the Law or the Prophets; I have not come to abolish them but to fulfill them." (Matthew 5:17, NIV)

Jesus came to earth and fulfilled the law and the prophets and established a New Covenant. Where the first Adam failed and sinned, the last Adam (Jesus) did not fail. Jesus fulfilled the law by living a sinless life, dying for us, being raised to life again, and making a way for us to be reconciled to Father God. Jesus satisfied all of the prophetic words that the prophets in the Old Testament had prophesied about the coming Messiah.

New Covenant

"...put on the new self, created to be like God in true righteousness and holiness." (Ephesians 4:24, NIV)

In the New Covenant in Jesus Christ, our new self is righteous and holy! As New Covenant, prophetic people, we are to be aligned with New Covenant values, not Old Covenant values. As Christians, we are to point fellow believers to their new self that is righteous and holy in Christ, not point them to their old sin nature.

New Covenant prophecy embraces the ministry of reconciliation

Old Covenant Prophecy	New Covenant Prophecy
Judged the people. (Ez. 18:30, Is. 1:4)	Encourages and directs people back to God in the ministry of reconciliation. (1 Cor. 14:1-4, 2 Cor. 5:17-19)

"...judgment without mercy will be shown to anyone who has not been merciful. Mercy triumphs over judgement." (James 2:13, NIV)

"Be merciful, just as your Father is merciful. Do not judge, and you will not be judged. Do not condemn, and you will not be condemned. Forgive, and you will be forgiven. Give, and it will be given to you. A good measure, pressed down, shaken together and running over, will be poured into your lap. For with the measure you use, it will be measured to you." (Luke 6:36-38, NIV)

As God's people, we are to release mercy. Our mandate is not to release judgment. This applies to us as we give prophetic words as well. We are to operate and release words of mercy instead of words of judgment.

> *"Therefore, if anyone is in Christ, the new creation has come: The old has gone, the new is here! All this is from God, who reconciled us to himself through Christ and gave us the ministry of reconciliation: that God was reconciling the world to himself in Christ, not counting people's sins against them. And he has committed to us the message of reconciliation."* (2 Corinthians 5:17-19, NIV)

In the New Covenant, we are given the ministry of reconciliation. Reconciliation can be defined as 'changing for the better a relationship between two or more persons'. We are challenged as Christians to draw people into a better relationship and friendship with Father God. This ministry of reconciliation is for all forms of ministry, including prophetic ministry.

According to this Scripture, the ministry of reconciliation is also about 'not counting their sins against them'. We will still sin, but in Jesus Christ, our sins are not counted against us. As prophetic people, our words should minister and assist in restoring right relationship between God and His people.

New Covenant prophecy calls us into our new identity and relationship with Jesus Christ

Old Covenant Prophecy	New Covenant Prophecy
Points to sin and calls for repentance and change of behaviour. (Ez. 18:30)	Points to Jesus calling for repentance and change in relationship. (Lk. 5:32, Gal. 4:4-7)
Old Covenant is a visitation culture where Holy Spirit visits the people. (1 Sam. 10:10, Gen. 41:38, 1 Sam. 16:13)	New Covenant is a habitation culture where Holy Spirit inhabits the people. (Jn. 14:16-18)

"But when the set time had fully come, God sent his Son, born of a woman, born under the law, to redeem those under the law, that we might receive adoption to sonship. Because you are his sons, God sent the Spirit of his Son into our hearts, the Spirit who calls out, "Abba, Father." So you are no longer a slave, but God's child; and since you are his child, God has made you also an heir." (Galatians 4:4-7, NIV)

"And I will ask the Father, and he will give you another advocate to help you and be with you forever—the Spirit of truth. The world cannot accept him, because it neither sees him nor knows him. But you know him, for he lives with you and will be in you.

I will not leave you as orphans; I will come to you."
(John 14:16-18, NIV)

"...God's kindness is intended to lead you to repentance."(Romans 2:4b, NIV)

Before Jesus Christ, God's people did not have the working of Holy Spirit within them. Holy Spirit was given to select people in the Old Testament: kings, priests, prophets, and other select individuals. Prior to Christ, the people were spiritually dead. They had the laws of God so that they could choose to obey God, but they were unable to follow the laws perfectly. Part of the role of the Old Testament prophet was to deliver a message from God to tell people when they were sinning as well as to enact judgment for their sin. The Old Testament prophets were the voice of God to the people. Today, we have the Bible to reveal to us how to obey and follow God, and we also have Holy Spirit to be the voice of God in our lives and lead us to repentance.

Since the Old Testament prophets were speaking on behalf of God, and the people did not have the Spirit of God within them, the penalty for the prophets speaking an inaccurate, prophetic word was death. Today, since we have Holy Spirit within us, anytime we hear a prophetic word spoken to us through another believer, we take this word to Holy Spirit that we might discern for ourselves the accuracy and validity of the prophetic word.

Romans 2:4 tells us that God's kindness is intended to lead us to repentance. Holy Spirit works out the sanctification process very uniquely for each person. As prophetic people, we call believers into New Covenant relationship with Father God, Jesus, and Holy Spirit. Then, we trust Jesus and Holy Spirit to be the ones to lead people to see their sin. This is not our job with the prophetic words we speak.

Prophets

"Before I formed you in the womb I knew you, before you were born I set you apart; I appointed you as a prophet to the nations." (Jeremiah 1:5, NIV)

"Now these are the gifts Christ gave to the church: the apostles, the prophets, the evangelists, and the pastors and teachers. Their responsibility is to equip God's people to do his work and build up the church, the body of Christ." (Ephesians 4:11-12)

A common question that arises with the discussion of the gift of prophecy and prophets is, "Do prophets exist today?" First of all, the label of 'prophet' was used to set a person apart in ministry in both the Old and the New Testament. Now, let's briefly discuss New Covenant prophets according to the passage in Ephesians and how that relates to someone who is named a prophet today. Generally, prophets are not often in a prominent position within the current, North American church. For this reason, we will focus on some common questions related to New Testament prophets.

What is a New Testament prophet?

The gift of prophecy is from Holy Spirit (1 Corinthians 12), and we can access it by desire (1 Corinthians 14:1). A true prophet is a gift to the church from Jesus Christ (Ephesians 4:11-12). This is a call from Him and is not something that we can choose for ourselves. According to

232

Ephesians 4, the prophet's responsibility is to equip God's people to do His work and build up the Body of Christ. Just because you have the gift of prophecy does not mean that you are a prophet.

The gift of prophecy and the call of a prophet are different and separate from each other. Someone called to be a prophet by Jesus will have the gift of prophecy and will operate within the guidelines of New Covenant prophecy as previously discussed. Sometimes, people who have named themselves a prophet believe that it is their right to deliver words of judgment and point out sin. However, a legitimate New Covenant prophet will not violate New Covenant values as they prophesy.

How can I operate as a prophet?

Ephesians 4 states that a prophet is given to the church to operate as one of five leaders within the church. Know that, if Jesus has called you to be a prophet, you cannot operate in this role until your church leadership recognizes you as a prophet <u>and</u> releases you to operate in this function. You will be able to operate as a prophet to the extent that your church leadership gives you permission. They will define what this looks like. Remember that the principle of submission to leadership is operable here and must be respected. Choose to submit to the leaders that God has placed within your church.

Be cautious of people who name themselves a prophet but seem to operate independently of a biblical community and are not in submission to leadership and no accountability. God values the Body of Christ and desires us to be in relationship operating together in unity (Ephesians 4:1-16). Notice that Ephesians 4 lists five

233

groups of people that build up the Body of Christ, *not* just the prophets in isolation.

If Jesus has called you as a prophet, it is unwise to announce this to others. Share this only with trusted friends. If Jesus wants you to operate as a prophet in your church, He will give you favour with the leadership, and they will promote you to the role and function of a prophet. Avoid self-promotion. Recognize that you may be called as a prophet, but if your church does not recognize you in this capacity or there is no structure within your church for the ministry of a prophet, you cannot operate as one. As prophetic people, it is vital that we remain in submission to our church leadership and operate in our prophetic gift or in our role as prophets as our leadership deems best.

Note: If this is a topic that interests you, and you would like to study the topic of prophets further, I highly recommend reading *School of the Prophets* by Kris Vallotton. Kris Vallotton offers a balanced view of what prophets are and what they are not. He provides foundational teaching on this topic and critical, advanced training.

Listening Exercise

Prophetic Practice

As you desire the gift of prophecy and want to grow your gift, you will need to practice giving prophetic words. This is where having a safe, prophetic community is crucial. Even if you only have one or two other individuals in your community, you will need safe people to risk with and speak out what you sense the Lord is saying to you for others. Remember that God may speak through your thoughts, feelings, and imagination, so His words will often feel like they are your own. Keep in mind that the only way to discover if it is God's voice or your own is by speaking it out and asking for feedback from the person you are giving the prophetic word to.

Any of the questions that you utilized in the previous Listening Exercises for yourself can be used to listen to God for others. Start by asking God questions for others while you are alone with Holy Spirit. Write down what you are sensing. After you are done writing, review what you have written to ensure that it lines up with the Bible and the character of God.

Here are some sample questions that you can use as you petition the Lord for a prophetic word for someone else:

- What do You love about their heart, God?
- What about them makes You smile?
- What Bible verse do they need in this season of their life?
- What is the song that You are currently singing over them (Zephaniah 3:17)?

Now deliver the prophetic word you have been given to the person and request their feedback. Specifically, ask them if they hear truth in the word. Was this something that they needed to hear at this time? Does the word answer a question that they have previously asked of the Lord or had in their heart? Do they feel strengthened, encouraged, and comforted? Does it minister to a need or cry of their heart? Does the word speak to who they are in Christ? Did the word impart healing and hope into their being? The bottom line is, do they sense that God was in this word?

As you grow in confidence, and as others are affirming that you are indeed hearing from God, begin to give prophetic words to others outside of your prophetic community. Do so with people who are open to the prophetic, with new Christians, even to those who may not yet know Jesus or who are strangers. If you know the person you are prophesying over, ask them to give you feedback. Be watchful for the opportunities Holy Spirit brings to speak into someone else's life and petition Him for those open doors to prophesy outside of your personal, prophetic community.

Going Deeper

Extra Practice

Endeavour to integrate prophecy into your life and make it part of your lifestyle of faith. Utilize questions to help you receive information from Holy Spirit. As you interact with others, be aware of and sensitive to the people that you are prophesying over and adjust your words so as to present them in such a way that they will be well received. Bring before Holy Spirit questions, not just for people you know, but also for people you don't know. Be sensitive to the doors Holy Spirit will open to speak to people, be they baby believers, seasoned Christians, unbelievers, or even strangers. If you know the person you are prophesying over, remember to ask them to provide feedback.

Here are some ideas to help you as you listen to Holy Spirit for others:

- Ask Holy Spirit to help you write an encouraging note for someone.
- Ask Holy Spirit how He is praying for a friend or family member. Call them and ask if you can pray for them.
- Ask Holy Spirit questions while you are visiting with someone (over coffee, dinner, etc.). Question Holy Spirit about what He loves about your friend. Tell them what Holy Spirit says.

If your word was accurate but was not received by the person, do not become discouraged. After your time together with the person, ask Holy Spirit how you could have done it differently. Learn from His suggestions. Also, realize that some people just don't want to receive prophetic words or don't know how to receive them. If they are resistant to your words, bless them and release them in their journey. However, if they are unsure about how to receive the word because receiving a prophetic word is new and possibly uncomfortable for them, ask them if they want to learn more about the gift of prophecy. Next, simply teach them as Holy Spirit leads you.

Finally, ask Holy Spirit to bring people to you that are hungry for prophetic words of blessing. Then, practice your gift of prophecy, bless others, and have fun!

The Eagle has Landed

Original painting by Deanna Oelke

"I, Jesus, have sent my angel to give you this testimony for the churches. I am the Root and the Offspring of David, and the bright Morning Star."
(Revelation 22:16, NIV)

The eagle in this picture represents the gift of prophecy. The gift of prophecy holds the key to unlocking mysteries and treasures in Heaven from God. Jesus – represented by the bright, morning star – is our high priest and is praying for God's will to be accomplished in our lives. The gift of prophecy flows out of Jesus' heart for us and speaks truth, hope, and love.

"The eagle has landed" is an expression used when something has been accomplished. My hope and desire is that the gift of prophecy will flow freely and purely through God's people and accomplish its purpose.

Chapter 12

How to Give a Prophetic Word to Others

As you are preparing yourself to hear God's voice for others, you may find it helpful to think through the process outlined in this chapter as you receive prophetic words from the Lord. If you are writing out a prophetic word for someone, it will be easy to consider these steps, for you will have time to ponder with Holy Spirit. If, however, you are delivering a prophetic word as you are receiving it from the Lord, you will be thinking, processing, and delivering quickly. This can involve multitasking as you are speaking the word to the person.

The whole process of receiving and delivering a word becomes easier with practice. Also, do not expect that Holy

Spirit will give you a prophetic word in the same way each time. Be open to whichever way He may want to show you something for another person. Trust Holy Spirit in these moments and follow His voice and leading.

Receiving a Prophetic Word from the Lord

God may choose to invade your space and give you a prophetic word for someone. God can do this in the following ways:

- A thought about a person that randomly comes into your mind
- An impression or a feeling about a person
- God being more obvious and saying, "I want to talk to you about someone."
- Another way that you know He speaks to you – be sensitive to His voice

Instead of dismissing the subtler ways that God may use to give you a prophetic word, actively interact with God and begin to dialogue with Him about the information. When you sense that God is giving you a word for someone else, ask Him, "Do you want me to speak this out now, later, or never?" Do not assume that because God is showing you something that you have to speak it out immediately. Be patient and wait for further direction, being sensitive to God's timing.

If God is showing you something negative about a person, you especially need to ask Him how He wants you to present it. Remember, we are to only speak out words that will strengthen, encourage, and comfort. This means that for each insight that is negative, you will need to rely on Holy Spirit to turn it into that freedom word that brings the redemption, resolution, and restoration that I talked about in Chapter 10. In addition, God may be showing you something about another person so that you can simply pray and intercede for them. He may not want you to speak out the prophetic word at all but use the insight He's given you to 'speak life' into the other person through prayer. Be obedient as the Lord directs you.

Once you have the gift of prophecy, you can also invade God's space and receive a prophetic word for nearly anyone. When you press in and ask the Lord for prophetic words for others, you may find it easier to start the conversation by asking Him a question. Once you become more practiced, you will just be able to ask God, "What would You like to say to this person?" and this will be enough of a lead in for Him to begin giving you information.

As I became more attuned to the voice of God and more familiar with my prophetic gift, I became more aware of biblical communities that were open to the prophetic as well as to those that were closed to the prophetic. When I sense a resistance to the prophetic, I often choose not to exercise my gift of prophecy. Yet, sometimes God has other ideas.

I remember one time when I was leaving a church service. In the midst of the people present, I had chosen not to use my prophetic gift or press in to the Lord for words for others. I was not interested in giving any words and was, quite frankly, feeling very introverted and did not want to interact with others. Nevertheless, God had a different agenda. Immediately, He invaded my space and gave me a vision with the complete interpretation for the worship leader. At that moment, the worship leader was on stage cleaning up in front of everyone who remained. My initial thought was, *"No, thank you, Lord!"*

I continued to walk out of the sanctuary thinking, *"If I don't deliver this prophetic word, God will ask someone else to deliver it."* God perceived my thoughts and quickly replied, *"Not with this word, Deanna. If you don't deliver it, he won't receive it."* This stopped me in my tracks.

The word was a great word. In fact, I would have wanted to receive it myself. Faced with the choice, I chose to be obedient and risk delivering this prophetic word even though I did not know the worship leader well or know if he would receive it. As I delivered the word to him, he was very emotional. I could see that there was something in the prophetic word that he needed to hear in that divinely appointed moment. I was very thankful that I had obeyed the voice of Holy Spirit.

Expanding the Prophetic Word

As you receive from Holy Spirit, continue to ask Him questions. Ask Him what the word means, what He is saying to this person on a deeper level, and if there is anything more He wants to show you. Press in to ensure that you receive all the information that Holy Spirit desires to give you.

If you are trying to expand on the prophetic word, but you are not getting more than one word, sentence, or simple picture, begin to speak out the little that you have heard or seen. Often, God will give more once you start speaking. Your step of faith in speaking out the little you have often unfolds more of the word. This method requires more boldness on your part. Then, as you are speaking, multitask and continue to ask God questions in your spirit as you are speaking. You may be listening to God and speaking to the person at the same time.

If you speak out the one word and don't receive any more from Holy Spirit, then trust that His desire was for you to give just a simple message to the other person. You can

244

present a simple, prophetic word like this: "I am just hearing the word 'boldness' for you. I am not sure what else God wants to say regarding this. Maybe you can ask the Lord what more He has to say." I have found that the simple, prophetic words are often remembered the easiest and can have more impact than longer words. Remember that even one single spoken word from the heart of God can accomplish exactly what He desires (Isaiah 55:11).

As I am receiving a prophetic word, I can occasionally sense that there is more to the prophetic word, but I cannot access it because Holy Spirit seems to be 'withholding' information from me. In these moments, I will tell the person that I sense that there is more to the prophetic word, and I then encourage them to journey with Holy Spirit to discover more information and details. This is less of a 'withholding' in relation to my being able to hear from God and more of an invitation to the person receiving the word to continue with Holy Spirit in relationship to discover the 'more'.

Delivering the Prophetic Word

Be mindful of your environment and be culturally relevant in how you present your prophetic word from the Lord. Is this person a Christian? If they are, is hearing from the Lord through the prophetic part of their 'normal'? Endeavour to present the word in a way that they will be able to best receive it. Not all Christians will be familiar with the prophetic. Thus, you may choose to stay away from words like 'prophecy' or 'prophetic' until you know what their understanding is.

If the person is a Christian, you can say something like this:

- "I sense that God is telling me something encouraging for you. Is it okay if I share it with you?"

If the person is not a Christian, here is an example of how you can present it:

- "I am a Christian (or follower of Jesus), and I believe that God still speaks to people today. I feel like He is telling me some encouraging things about you. May I share them with you?"

I have found that it is important when you lead in to giving a prophetic word to say somewhere in your introduction that you have something <u>encouraging</u> to share with the other person. I discovered this as I would approach people by saying, "I sense that God is showing me something about you." Shocked and terrified expressions told me that they were thinking that God had shown me something bad about them or a sin of some sort. They were most likely defaulting to an Old Covenant understanding of how prophecy was delivered, and they were not responding from an awareness of New Covenant guidelines. With a simple introduction and using the word 'encouraging', you will be indirectly introducing people to New Covenant, prophetic values and ease their minds about receiving the word God has laid on your heart.

Occasionally, the person's belief system will prevent them from receiving the word. Some people do not believe that God speaks today, and they do not believe in the gift of prophecy. You will encounter times where you cannot perceive this before you give a prophetic word. If the person does not respond positively towards you, do not become discouraged. Bless them anyway. Keep being obedient as the Lord prompts you to share encouraging, prophetic words with others.

Releasing Prophetic Words

Your words should push people into God. We want people to be dependent on God, not on us. Think of how you can end your prophetic word so that you very simply tell them what the next step(s) are such as, "Take these words to the Lord and see what He says about it." With a statement like this, you are communicating that God desires to speak to them personally, that they have access to God, what they can do next in waiting on Him, and that you are not the expert on their life – God is.

Once you have delivered a prophetic word, your job is probably done. Your responsibility now is to release others in their journey. If God has something more for you to do, Holy Spirit will tell you.

People will have varied responses to your prophetic words. By giving prophetic words, I have made new friends, journeyed deeply with some people, scared other people off who were afraid of what I would 'see', and offended those who could not receive the word in the right spirit. Whatever the response, it is important to process the exchange with Holy Spirit afterwards. Let Him be your teacher regarding your delivery and any adjustments you may need to make. Holy Spirit may also have you continue to pray for the person. Be faithful to pray for them if He prompts you to do so, and continue to interact with them in providing prophetic words if Holy Spirit leads.

Many times, you will not know if your prophetic words come to pass, and this can be hard. In these instances, you need to actively engage your faith and trust that Holy Spirit will continue to work in that other person's life to accomplish all that He plans and purposes. Don't let not knowing the end result discourage you.

However, this is another reason why prophetic community is so important. You need to see in at least some people's lives if your prophetic words are bearing fruit. Being involved in your prophetic community gives you that opportunity to track what God has given you and how the word is being fulfilled. Remember, some fruit grows and manifests with time. You may only see the fulfillment of your prophetic words if you are journeying with people over time.

Prophetic Words to Avoid

I think it is wise to take some time to touch on prophetic words to avoid. I occasionally come across people who are resistant to the prophetic because they have been hurt through those not stewarding their gift well. Often, they have been hurt through someone who has not operated in New Covenant values and sin was pointed out or they felt judged. Whatever the circumstances, the content of the prophetic word was hurtful or negative.

Avoid futuristic, prophetic words that give specific direction

Words should not be *specifically* directive (E.g. God wants you to quit your job and move to Africa). Although you may have a sense of a direction that God wants to take that person in the future, it is wise to show restraint in delivering an exact directive. Instead, present the prophetic word in a way that requires the person to press in to God to receive that specific direction straight from Him.

- Example: "I sense that there is something for you related to traveling overseas. Ask the Lord for more about this and what this looks like. Trust His leading and His timing."

<u>Avoid prophetic words that give dates, mates, or predict babies</u>

You can well imagine that prophetic words that predict a timeline, someone's mate, or predicts the birth of a baby can be very hurtful if you end up being wrong. It is wise to stay away from words of this nature.

The Battle Against Pride

"God opposes the proud but gives grace to the humble." (James 4:6b)

I believe one of the main ways that Satan tries to ensnare people with the gift of prophecy is through pride. Once others know that you have the gift of prophecy, they may come to you to hear from God. This is not necessarily a bad thing. However, it is important to ask Holy Spirit how to respond to each individual when you are asked for a word.

When you perceive that people are coming to you instead of going to God for themselves, gently push them toward God by encouraging them to go to Him directly to receive a word. In this way, you can help others from short-changing themselves in their relationship with God and spur them on to develop greater intimacy with Him.

The gift of prophecy has a 'wow' factor to it. When people recognize that you have the gift of prophecy, they will be watching you. Many people will assume that the gift of

249

prophecy means you are also a very spiritual person, that you have good character, and you enjoy a great relationship with God. The fact is, a person can have the gift of prophecy but still have flaws in their character and issues in their personal relationship with God. Holy Spirit gives the gift freely without the condition of being spiritually mature. Our desire as a prophetic people must be to not only speak the words of God but to *live* the Word of God.

Operating in the gift of prophecy is a balance between possessing the confidence in knowing you have the gift of prophecy and that you hear from God and walking in humility knowing you are not perfect and that you will make mistakes. People may assume that when their prophetic gift matures, they will be 100% accurate in delivering all their prophetic words. I have found that this is not the case. Remember, we prophesy in part. I believe that God does this on purpose to keep us in a posture of humility. In realizing that we can make mistakes, we become dependent on Him instead of dependent on our gift. When we remain in love and stay within the guidelines of encouraging, comforting, and edifying others, even when we hear incorrectly, our prophetic words will still be a source of encouragement to the person receiving it.

As you see your prophetic gift growing, I encourage you to pray this simple prayer: "God, don't let my prophetic gift outgrow my character." Let us be a holy, prophetic people whose hearts desire to lift up and glorify the name of Jesus in all that we say and do!

Listening Exercise

Treasure Box

Once people begin to operate in their gift of prophecy, I consistently hear them say how difficult it is to prophesy over people that they know well. When you receive information from Holy Spirit about a close friend or family member, it is easy to second-guess yourself and question, "Is this Holy Spirit, or am I just thinking this because I know this person so well?"

Think of friends and family members that are open to the prophetic and that you want to give a prophetic word to. Write each of their names on separate, small pieces of paper and place them in a little box. Pick a name out of the box and, without looking at whose name you have drawn, begin to ask Holy Spirit questions about the person. Then, write out a prophetic word for them. Once you are finished writing it down, look at the name that you have picked.

Next, it is important to process with Holy Spirit. Do so by asking the following questions:

1. Does this word 'fit' the person?

2. Seek Holy Spirit as to what to do with the word.
    *   Does He want you to use it to pray for the person?
    *   Does He want you to give it to the person? If the answer is "yes", ask Him when is the best timing to do so. If the answer is "no", wait on Him for further direction as to what He wants to do.

Repeat this process as often as you like.

Glory Mountain

Original painting by Deanna Oelke

"Come, and let us go up to the mountain of the Lord, to the house of the God of Jacob; He will teach us His ways, And we shall walk in His paths."...
(Micah 4:2, NKJV)

I painted this picture during worship at a conference. I wanted to depict the need to be like children in order to enter the Kingdom of Heaven.

The sword in the boy's hand represents the sword of the Spirit – the Word of the Lord. To follow the right-path is our own choice. A door in the mountain leads into the presence of the Lord. There is a small, heralding angel in the clouds releasing a clarion call to all believers.

Chapter 13

Stewarding Prophetic Words Given to You

Hopefully at this point in your Deeper journey, you have been experiencing it with a prophetic community, and you have received multiple prophetic words spoken over you. You might be thinking, *"What do I do with these words now?"* In this chapter, you will learn some tools to help you in knowing what the next steps could be. If you have not been journeying with a prophetic community and have not received outside prophetic words, you can still use your personal times with the Lord when He has spoken to you directly and steward those words in the same way.

Before we begin to talk about how to journey with prophetic words and the spoken word of God (prophecies or Holy Spirit's voice directly to you), let's talk about how you journey with the written Word of God: the Bible. There are times when you hear or read a Bible verse, and it seems to leap off of the page. You feel the truth of what you have read, and you experience the Bible as the active and living word of God doing a work in your spirit even as you are hearing it. Your part is simply to submit to God and receive the truth as it floods your spirit.

Then, there are times that you read a Bible verse that is a promise of God like the one found in Romans 8:28: *"...God causes everything to work together for the good of those who love God and are called according to his purpose for them."* You know that this is truth, but your situation in that moment of your life is not good, and you may be experiencing the reality of the enemy stealing from you and destroying parts of you (John 10:10). How do you respond when the truth of God's written Word does not line up with the facts of your life?

- Choose to activate your faith and continue to believe that what God has said in the Bible is truth and is true for you (2 Corinthians 11: 1, 6).
- Trust in God and His character – that He is good (Psalm 136:1), that He loves you (Ephesians 2:4-5), and that He is for you and not against you (Romans 8:31).
- Trust God's timing and that He has a plan for the larger vision of your life (Jeremiah 29:11).
- Pray in cooperation with the truth of God's Word to be manifested in your life (2 Corinthians 6:1-2, Romans 8:25).

- Set your sights on God (Psalm 121:1-2) and renew your mind in His promises (Romans 12:2).

Journeying with prophetic words compared to the written Word of God has some similarities, but it also has some differences. One of the main differences in stewarding prophetic words compared to stewarding Bible verses is how you 'hold' the word. Let me explain...

The Bible is truth. When God says in the Bible that He will work all things together for good for those who love him and are called according to his purpose (Romans 8:28), you know that this is truth. You can go boldly before His throne of grace with confidence saying, "God, I love you, and I am called according to your purpose for me, so I am asking that You touch this situation in my life. You've said that You will work all things together for my good. Therefore, I am asking You to turn this current situation in my life into something good. Thank you!" God cannot deny Himself, and He cannot go against His written Word. You can hold the promises in His written Word tightly – with a closed hand – and cling to them as truth.

Prophecy, on the other hand, can be truth as well, but it should be held loosely with an open hand. Remember that one of the main truths about prophecy is that a prophetic word is *partial* information (1 Corinthians 13:9). Prophecy is just one puzzle piece and not the whole picture. When you first hear a prophetic word that is visionary and for the future, you will probably have an idea as to how you think it will work out in your life. God invariably has a unique and sometimes very different way of working out that word in our lives, for God's ways are not our ways (Isaiah 55:8). We can do our part to move ourselves towards a prophetic word from the Lord, but there will always be an element of letting go and trusting God to do His part – to move in His way and in His time. Don't control and manipulate the circumstances in your life to force a prophetic word to happen. Do your part but also step back and give God room to do the miraculous in your life!

In the same way that you have been making certain that the prophetic words you deliver to others are encouraging, strengthening, and comforting, measure each prophetic word that others speak over you with this same spiritual principle. Do not allow others that are prophesying over you to point out your sin or tell you what you are doing wrong. Instead, ensure that you are receiving prophetic words that encourage and build you up. In doing this, you set good boundaries for yourself as you are receiving prophetic words. If someone begins to point out sin or you feel that the word they have for you is discouraging, you have permission to stop him or her and say something like this: "Can you stop, please. I believe that the gift of prophecy is for the encouragement, strengthening, and comfort of God's people. I am not feeling encouraged by your prophetic word, and I am not interested in hearing any more."

Remember that *you* are responsible for stewarding the prophetic words that others give you. This means taking every encouraging word to Holy Spirit to ask Him what He would like to say to you regarding that word. If you haven't started already, consider writing down both what Holy Spirit is speaking to you and the prophetic words that you receive from others. Writing down the words will keep you from forgetting them and will also help you to easily review what the Lord has said.

Consider the following as you review your prophetic words with the Lord:

Prophecy Must Be Weighed

"Do not quench the Spirit. Do not treat prophecies with contempt but test them all; hold on to what is good." (1 Thessalonians 5:19-21, NIV)

Paul exhorts us in these verses to test every prophecy. We test prophecy against the truth of Scripture and the unchangeable and steadfast character of God and through sharing your word with trusted, prophetic friends and leaders for additional insight and counsel. While every believer can flow in a general grace of the prophetic gift, none walk in an authority of infallibility. We are all prone to making mistakes. Almost everyone has experienced a situation where they believed that God spoke only to find out later that He hadn't. Notice that Paul wants us to test every *thing*, not every *one*. Our job is to take every *thing* that is spoken over us to God and using godly discernment to test its truth.

Testing a prophetic word involves testing the details. And it doesn't have to be an 'all or nothing' approach. Hold onto the parts of the word that are good. Leave the rest. Holy Spirit will show you what you need to keep and what you need to discard.

Test each prophetic word yourself but also share your word with others. When you share your words with others, it is important that you share them with trusted people who know you and with those who understand prophecy. It is essential that these people not treat your prophecy with contempt. The purpose for sharing with others under these guidelines is so that God can bring forth additional discernment and revelation as well as confirm what you have already heard for yourself.

Just as you would watch for supernatural fruit when God has personally spoken to you in your own time with Him, watch for supernatural fruit regarding the prophetic words you receive from others. Do you feel a witness inside as to its truth? Do you feel life being infused into your being? Are fruits of the Spirit manifested because of the word coming forth? Does hope rise up within you when you first hear the prophetic word? If you do, this is a measure of good fruit. Remember to keep in mind that some fruit grows over time. This is where writing your prophetic words down is helpful for going back, revisiting, and seeing which ones have come to pass or have borne fruit. Testing prophetic words always involves examining the word for supernatural fruit.

Prophecy Requires Us to Engage Faith

Does this prophetic word stir a desire within you? Do you want this to happen in your life? If yes, pray in agreement with Holy Spirit for the words to come to pass. Remember that Holy Spirit is praying that the will of Father God be manifested in your life (Romans 8:26-27). You may have this desire because Holy Spirit first had this desire for you and placed it in your heart! Occasionally, Christians may think if they have a personal, heart's desire for God to do something in their lives that it is somehow selfish. That is not necessarily the case. If the prophetic word sparks a longing deep within your heart, *and* this heart's desire is in line with Scripture, then pray for it to happen. This is not at all selfish. The reality is that God wants to do <u>immeasurably more</u> for you than you can ever ask or imagine (Ephesians 3:20).

Prophecy May Require Action

"Timothy, my son, I am giving you this command in keeping with the prophecies once made about you, so that by recalling them you may fight the battle well."
(1 Timothy 1:18, NIV)

You may find it beneficial at this point to review Chapter 8 on <u>Stewarding Truth</u>. Many of the principles in this chapter's teaching are applicable here.

Different types of words require different kinds of action. These words are divided into four categories.

<u>A 'now' word</u>: The easiest prophetic words to journey with are the words that are for right now. These are the prophetic words that, when you hear them, you feel the truth of the word instantly, and your part is to just receive it and allow it to wash over your spirit and your mind. In doing so, you permit the word to actively do the work that Holy Spirit desires. In the 'now' words, there is an immediate work that the Lord does that we just need to be open and submissive to. There is not much stewardship beyond just receiving from the Lord.

<u>An identity word</u>: If the prophetic word is a truth about who you are, you can use it in the same way you would 'fight the battle' with a Bible verse. Activate your faith and believe that this is truth for your life even if you can't see it in the natural. Be transformed by the renewing of your mind. Take all of your thoughts captive to the obedience of Christ. You choose to agree with God about who you are in order to withstand the negative and make any changes that Holy Spirit directs you to.

261

A healing word: You may sense, feel, or hear the healing in a prophetic word. Press in to Holy Spirit, Jesus, or Father God to allow the completion of the work of healing in your life. Is there something more that He wants to say? Is there something that you need to process in the presence of Holy Spirit? Do you need to utilize the principles of combating lies from the enemy? Open your heart, mind, and body to receive the healing God has for you.

A visionary word: You may receive a word that speaks of things for the future. Is there something that you can do to practically move towards this prophetic word for it to happen? If so, engage with Holy Spirit, working with Him to plan and begin taking those steps forward while holding the prophetic word loosely with an open hand. You will probably have an idea of how this future word could unfold in your life, but God's ways are not our ways (Isaiah 55:8), so you will need to be sensitive to His direction and redirection. Do your part, stay tuned in to Holy Spirit, and allow God to do His part in the way that He wants to.

Prophecy is Partial Information

"For we know in part and we prophesy in part."
(1 Corinthians 13:9, NIV)

Do not make any major decisions on one prophetic blessing alone. If you have a prophetic word that points to making a major decision, ask the Lord for more information, petition Him for His timing, wait for confirmation, and seek out wise counsel from others.

Prophecy May Take Time

"For the revelation awaits an appointed time; it speaks of the end and will not prove false. Though it linger, wait for it; it will certainly come and will not delay." (Habakkuk 2:3, NIV)

Waiting can be hard, particularly when you are excited about something. This can be especially so when God fulfills a prophetic word slower than what we would want or expect. Yet, God is very patient. He yearns for us to live our lives with an eternal perspective. Therefore, He may even choose to fulfill a prophetic word on the other side of eternity when we die and enter Heaven. Trust God, trust His ways, and trust His timing.

What If a Prophetic Word Never Happens?

The emotional journey of a prophetic word not being fulfilled can be difficult, especially if it is something that you have long desired, earnestly hoped for, and petitioned and prayed for. If you make *love* and *relationship* with the Trinity your goal as you journey with a prophetic word instead of the actual fulfillment of that word, you will avoid intense disappointment if the word does not come to pass. A prophetic word not happening should not jeopardize your relationship with God. If an unfulfilled word does end up negatively affecting your relationship with God, then there is a problem in where you have placed your hope. Our hope should be placed in the Lord first and foremost.

Let us consider some possible reasons as to why words may not come to pass:

- There is a human factor in prophetic words – we are not perfect. Even though the word may be encouraging, the person prophesying may have communicated information that was from him or herself. Good people can deliver incorrect words. An incorrect word does not mean that the person is 'bad'. Remember that 1 Thessalonians 5:19-21 encourages us to test prophetic words, not prophetic people.

- A prophetic word may be active just for a season. Other people may need to cooperate for the word to happen, or there was action on your part that was necessary. If you feel you may have missed an opportunity with the Lord, ask Him for another chance. Our God is full of grace.

- Occasionally, God allows a prophetic promise to die in order that it may produce more seeds in our life and a plentiful harvest (John 12:24). God is not necessarily finished with the word! Put the word aside and ask Him to let you know when you are supposed to engage with it again.

- Sometimes, it is more important to God to show us our priorities than to fulfill a prophetic word. Above everything, we are to desire God first. As you move forward into a prophetic word that you dearly want to happen in your life, what if at the end of the journey all you have is God? Is having God enough for you? God desires to be first in your life.

- God may be more concerned about the journey than the word being fulfilled. Instead, in His wisdom, God's purpose to grow character within you takes precedence and priority above the spoken word. There may be details about yourself that He wants to reveal and work on. Submit the process to God, not only the result of a word fulfilled.

In journeying with any prophetic words, your default should always be following the lead of Holy Spirit. He is your guide and your companion. Trust Him and the ways He is working out everything for your good.

Listening Exercise

Processing Your Prophetic Word

Take a prophetic word that you have received from someone to line up with the points taught in this chapter. Try to choose a word that is longer. Process with Holy Spirit. If you don't have a prophetic word from someone, use a word that Holy Spirit has directly spoken to you.

Going Deeper

Extra Practice

One of my good friends loves to go 'Prayer Shopping'. Whenever she is going shopping for a birthday present, she involves Holy Spirit in the process. She follows His lead as to what to buy, and then she asks Him questions as to why He chose that specific item. I love getting presents from this friend because they always come with a prophetic word. As a result, every time I see the gift, I am reminded of the word of encouragement that God gave me through her.

Try going 'Prayer Shopping' for a friend! Choose to bless someone spontaneously with a gift accompanied with a prophetic word.

Kingdom of Heaven

Original painting by Deanna Oelke

"Blessed are the poor in spirit, for theirs is the kingdom of heaven." (Matthew 5:3, NIV)

This young lady sees her need for God. She is coming with empty and open hands, ready to receive from Him. She knows that, when she seeks Him, she will find Him. She has one goal – to love her God with all of her heart, soul, and mind.

God is represented in her hands with the Trinity symbol. The Kingdom of God flows out of this divine interaction and is represented by the symbolism of the butterflies, feathers, and the jewels.

Chapter 14

Words of Wisdom
and Words of Knowledge

"Now to each one the manifestation of the Spirit is given for the common good. To one there is given through the Spirit a <u>message of wisdom</u>, to another a <u>message of knowledge</u> by means of the same Spirit." (1 Corinthians 12:7-8, NIV)[13]

Holy Spirit is so extravagant! You may find that, while you simply exercise your gift of prophecy, Holy Spirit begins to give you other gifts. It often happens that, as people are

---

[13] (Emphasis mine)

operating in the gift of prophecy, they begin moving in words of wisdom or words of knowledge without even asking or desiring these gifts from Holy Spirit. In fact, the message of wisdom and message of knowledge are gifts from Holy Spirit that complement the gift of prophecy.

As I began to grow in my prophetic gift, Holy Spirit began to give me words of knowledge and words of wisdom. I began to see how beautifully these gifts flowed together with prophecy and provided a full and more complete message. It could have been easy for me to strive to operate in all three gifts each time I was to prophesy. Instead, I chose and still choose to remain in the simplicity of following Holy Spirit's lead and allowing Him to form the prophetic word and any other gift or ministry as He desires.

In this chapter, the teaching around these gifts will be practical in nature. The focus will remain on the gift of prophecy but will examine how words of knowledge and words of wisdom compliment the prophetic gift.

A Message/Word of Knowledge

Definition: Supernatural insight or understanding by revelation. This is information that you could not have received on your own; God gives you this information.

Biblical examples:

- Ananias in the conversion of Paul (Acts 9:10-12)
- Cornelius in finding Peter, who then was instrumental in introducing Holy Spirit to the Gentiles (Acts 10)

This gift works very well with the gift of prophecy. A message of supernatural knowledge communicates to the person, "God sees you!" Frequently, a message of knowledge opens up a person's spirit so that there are no walls or defence mechanisms. Then, a prophetic word communicating the truth and the love of Father God for the person is that much more powerful.

Words of knowledge can be showy. They carry a factor of: "Wow! How did you know that about me?" Keep your focus on the work that Holy Spirit wants to do in the person you are ministering to. Choose to operate in love and humility.

When I receive a word of knowledge about a person, I press in to Holy Spirit to find out how He wants me to use the information, and if He wants me to speak it out. I recall one time being invited to a Bible study with a group of ladies that I did not know. At the end of the study, we were moving into a time of prophesying over each other. It was one lady's turn to receive prophetic words. As I was asking Holy Spirit what He wanted to say, I immediately had a vision of her being abused by men. I knew that I could not speak out the rawness of what I saw. My thought was that it could be incredibly embarrassing for this to be revealed to the group. I pressed deeply in to Holy Spirit to receive wisdom for its delivery. This is what He told me to say: "God knows that you have not been treated well by men in the past [the word of knowledge graciously communicated]. Jesus wants to reveal Himself as a gentleman to you [the prophetic message]." The prophetic word then carried a word of wisdom as to how she could practically interact with Jesus to position herself to learn from Him as a gentleman. This lady needed to know that God saw the hurt of her past, He cared for her, and now He wanted to heal her through Jesus.

I remember another time I was teaching a small group of young girls how to hear God's voice. As we began listening to God for each other, I saw for one girl a vision of Jesus bouncing around like Tigger from the Winnie-the-Pooh stories. I could have very easily dismissed this as my crazy imagination and waited for something serious from Holy Spirit. In faith, I decided to speak out what I saw, and this is what unfolded:

"I see Jesus bouncing like Tigger."

The girls all gasped and looked at each other, their eyes wide open. I knew that something was up; God was somehow in that seemingly silly vision. The girls quickly told me that, earlier that evening when the girls were talking amongst themselves, this girl had said that her friends had nicknamed her "Tigger". God had their attention!

I then received the interpretation to the vision and knew why Jesus looked like Tigger.

"Jesus knows you so perfectly, and He wants to relate to you in a way that you will understand."

A word of wisdom followed as to how she could practically engage in relationship with Jesus that would allow Him to reveal Himself to her in a personal way.

A Message/Word of Wisdom

Definition: Supernatural wisdom versus human or worldly wisdom; seeing life from God's perspective. The gift of wisdom is the application of knowledge that God gives you.

"But the wisdom from above is first of all pure. It is also peace loving, gentle at all times, and willing to

yield to others. It is full of mercy and the fruit of good deeds. It shows no favoritism and is always sincere." (James 3:17)

Where a word of knowledge opens a person's spirit, and the gift of prophecy delivers a personal message from God, a word of wisdom gives instruction as to what to do next. This gift is a supernatural perspective to understanding how to accomplish God's will in a given situation. This gift could involve having a sense of divine direction that imparts purpose and confidence in the decisions you have to make and/or being led by Holy Spirit to act appropriately and in a specific manner within the situation.

You will know when you have been given a message of wisdom because it does not come from your own experiences or what you know. Many times, a word of wisdom will even teach you in the situation, bringing enlightenment and new understanding along with operational strategies. The Bible speaks so much about the benefit of wisdom. Eagerly desire this gift and pray for wisdom when you see that you have need of it.

There is a richness that is found in the wisdom from Heaven. Back when I began to receive words of wisdom, I knew that it flowed from the gift of wisdom because what was given did not come from my own head knowledge or from my own personal experiences. It was a supernatural impartation that could only come from a divine source. Often, when I receive a word of wisdom, my internal reaction is: *"This is good!"* I frequently find that I learn just as much from a word of wisdom that I am delivering as the person that I am speaking it to.

_____

As you are prophesying, you may very well begin to naturally move in the gifts of knowledge and of wisdom, delivering words and messages that can only come from God. The essence of prophesying is simply following Holy Spirit's lead. Be sensitive to how He is leading you, and process with Holy Spirit even as you are delivering a word so that you can flow in His Spirit and operate in whatever gift He desires. I also hope and pray that, as you journey with Holy Spirit and conform more and more to the likeness of Jesus, you will be a prophetic voice of love, hope, truth, and healing for the world and for the Body of Christ, operating in *all* the gifts Holy Spirit has for you for God's glory.

Listening Exercise
Practicing Words of Knowledge

The message of knowledge, like the gift of prophecy can be practiced. Firstly, pray for this gift. Then, as you interact with a person, ask Holy Spirit for information that you could only obtain from Him. Next, ask the person questions to find out if the information is accurate. Let me give you an example of how this can be practically done.

You are at a gathering of people. You find yourself interacting with a woman that you do not know very well. As you wait on Holy Spirit for a word of knowledge, you sense that she has a son that plays basketball. Begin, then, to ask the lady questions to find out if you have indeed received a word of knowledge from Holy Spirit: "Do you have children? Does your son play sports? What kind of sports does he play?" and so on and so forth. Through your questions posed through conversation, you can easily confirm whether you have heard correctly.

The purpose of practicing receiving words of knowledge is not to minister or prophesy but for you to grow in your gift. As you recognize and gain confidence in the fact that you are moving in this gift, you can then begin to step out in faith and boldness and use it alongside your gift of prophecy.

Alabaster Jar

Original painting by Deanna Oelke

"Meanwhile, Jesus was in Bethany at the home of Simon, a man who had previously had leprosy. While he was eating, a woman came in with a beautiful alabaster jar of expensive perfume and poured it over his head." (Matthew 26:6-7)

I was inspired to paint Julie Meyer's song "Alabaster Box". In this song, she sings about giving all that she has just as the woman from Bethany did in breaking the alabaster jar upon Jesus. As I listen to the song, I often imagine what the different fragrances of my offerings to Jesus would look like. This is the idea that I tried to capture in this painting.

Chapter 15

Going Deeper

As you finish reading *Deeper,* having engaged in formal listening times with Holy Spirit along the way, it is now up to you as to how you will foster your deeper, heart-to-heart relationship with Holy Spirit. You are also responsible for the growth and stewardship of your prophetic gift. Here are some ideas to help you continue to grow in your prophetic gift:

1. Practice hearing God's voice for yourself and others.
   - Faithfully steward what the Lord gives you. Act on what He shows you.

2. Ask the Lord for increase.
   - James 4:2b (NKJV): *"...you do not have because you do not ask."*

- Ask and be open to God revealing Himself in new ways.

3. Hang out with those who love the prophetic.
   - Learn from those who know and practice the gift of prophecy and build relationships with them.
   - It is wise to be a part of the Body of Christ, as this is whom the gift of prophecy is for. Do not isolate yourself.

4. Seek out opportunities within your church to use your prophetic gift.

I hope and pray that your relationship with the Holy Trinity has grown stronger and deeper as you have engaged with Holy Spirit. Additionally, I trust that you have found a biblical community where you are free to be yourself and grow in your gifts.

If you have found this Deeper journey transformative, you may want to consider leading others through the Deeper experience. Deeper Leader and Participant Manuals are specifically designed for you to practically lead a group of willing participants into hearing God, operating in the gift of prophecy, and fostering a prophetic community. The leader manuals are very practical in nature and are laid out in such a way that anyone can pick up and utilize them even if they haven't led a group before. The principles and teaching within the manuals are the same as what you have learned and practiced in *Deeper – Heart to Heart with Holy Spirit.*

I encourage you, as you continue experiencing relationship with Father God, Jesus, and Holy Spirit, to share your stories. Your testimonies of God's goodness and love will encourage others in their own personal relationships with the Lord. This will encourage them to taste and see for themselves that the Lord is indeed a good God!

"To him who is able to keep you from stumbling and to present you before his glorious presence without fault and with great joy—to the only God our Savior be glory, majesty, power and authority, through Jesus Christ our Lord, before all ages, now and forevermore! Amen." (Jude 1:24-25, NIV)

About the Author

Deanna Oelke

I grew up in a Baptist home and was raised by parents that lived their Christian life authentically. This strong, biblical upbringing was foundational for my Christian maturity and for Holy Spirit to lead me into my spiritual gifts.

As an adult, I learned how to hear God's voice for myself. Within a small community of Christian women, I received the gift of prophecy from Holy Spirit. We met weekly and practiced listening to God and prophesying to each other. I experienced Holy Spirit as my personal mentor, teacher, guide, and counsellor. After being in this community for a number of months, I experienced dramatic spiritual growth, transformation, and inner healing.

This experience of prophetic community motivated a friend and me to create a prophetic ministry. We taught men, women, and children how to hear God's voice for themselves and others, as well as how to steward the gift of prophecy. Within our community and prophetic culture, people experienced an enriched relationship with God and dynamic, spiritual transformation.

Eventually, God led me to reintegrate into established, Christian institutions. Leading Deeper communities is one way that God has provided opportunities for me to equip fellow Christians in hearing God's voice, to operate in the gift of prophecy, and to equip leaders in creating prophetic communities.

My prayer is that you will experience true, biblical community within your Deeper experience. I pray that you may come to know practically, as well as through experience, the love of Christ that far surpasses mere knowledge, and that you may be made complete with all the fullness of life and power that comes from God. My hope is that God will accomplish infinitely more than you could ever ask or imagine! (Ephesians 3:18-20)

Deeper Materials

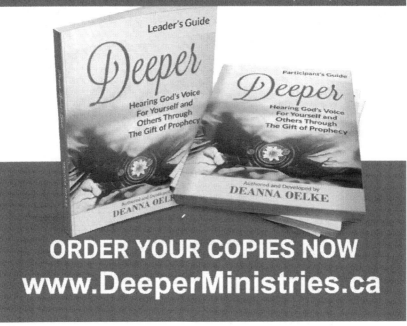

Appendix ~ Resources

There are so many books and resources on prophecy. If you are interested in deepening your knowledge on the subject, I would suggest the following authors and ministries:

Graham Cooke is one of my favourite authors. If you are interested in reading a good book on the gift of prophecy, I would recommend *Approaching the Heart of Prophecy.* Graham's soaking CDs are wonderful as well. His website is: brilliantbookhouse.com

Kris Vallotton is a great teacher. His website offers a variety of audio teaching, DVDs, books, and free podcasts from Bethel Church. You can find him at: kvministries.com

Shawn Bolz is a spiritual adviser, producer, media personality, and minister. He is passionate about seeing individuals and groups learn how to be the most connected and best version of themselves. Shawn has been a pioneer in ministry, including the prophetic movement, since he was in his teens. His focus on having a genuine relationship with God, of creativity through entertainment, and on social justice have sent him around the world to meet with churches, CEOs, entertainers, and world leaders. His website is: bolzministries.com

Streams Ministries is a great, equipping ministry. Founded by John Paul Jackson, Streams Ministries is an in-depth, training ministry that exists to nurture individuals in the art of hearing God, dreams, visions, and the realms of the supernatural. They seek to mentor those with revelatory gifts so they might grow in deeper intimacy with God. Good resources and courses are offered online from their website: streamscanada.com and streamsministries.com

Inner Healing:

Ellel Ministries is a non-denominational, Christian ministry that began in England in 1986 and is now established in over 20 countries around the world. They look to serve the Body of Christ in two main ways: offering personal prayer ministry to those in need, and training and equipping people so that they can help others more effectively. Their website is: ellel.org

22757100R00167

Made in the USA
Columbia, SC
04 August 2018